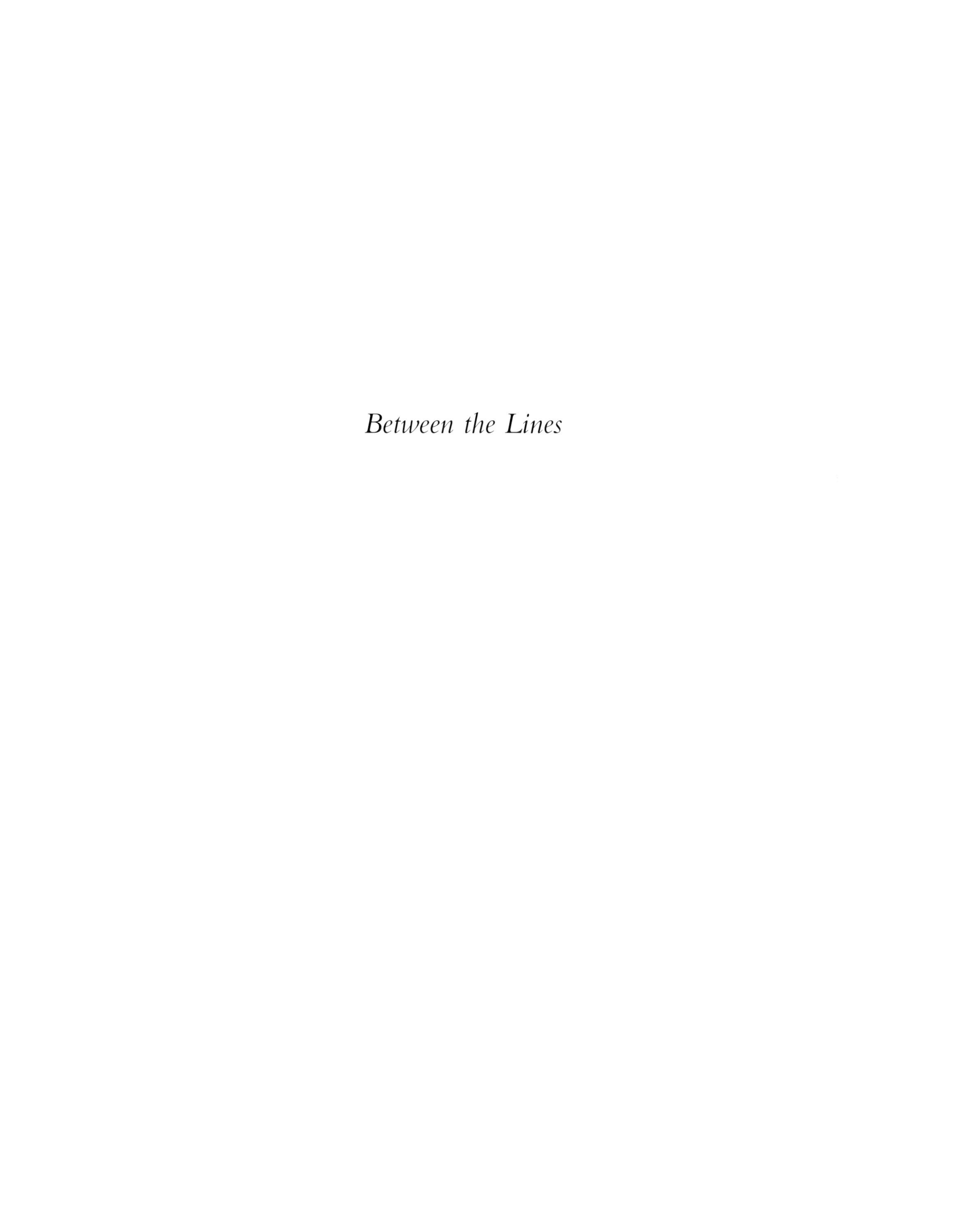

Between the Lines

Between the Lines

Photographs from the
National Vietnam Veterans Memorial

THOMAS F. MORRISSEY

With Forewords by
JAN CRAIG SCRUGGS *and* ADRIAN CRONAUER

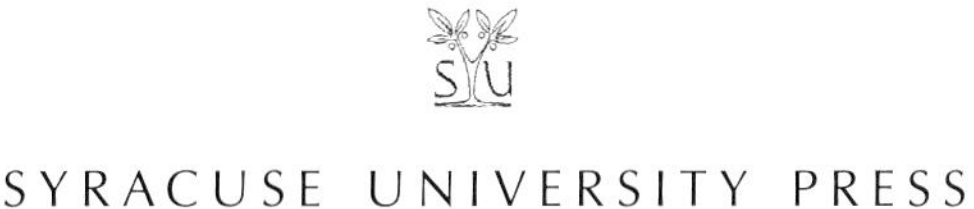

SYRACUSE UNIVERSITY PRESS

First Edition 2000

00 01 02 03 04 05   6 5 4 3 2 1

Individual images, as well as the complete exhibition of the photographs and text contained in *Between the Lines: Photographs from the National Vietnam Veterans Memorial* are available to museums and organizations. On-line information: http://www.artznet.com/btl.htm; E-mail: morrissey@artznet.com

The paper used in this publication meets the minimum requirements of American National Standard for Information Sciences—Permanence of Paper for Printed Library Materials, ANSI Z39.48-1984. ∞™

Library of Congress Cataloging-in-Publication Data

Morrissey, Thomas F.
Between the lines: photographs from the National Vietnam Veterans Memorial / Thomas F. Morrissey; with forewords by Jan Craig Scruggs and Adrian Cronauer.—1st ed.
p. cm.
ISBN 0-8156-0591-9 (cloth : alk. paper)
1. Vietnam Veterans Memorial (Washington, D.C.)—Pictorial works. I. Title.
DS559.83.W18M67 2000
959.704'36—dc21   99-087050

Manufactured in the United States of America

To my mother for all her prayers while I was away,
to Lance for his sacrifice, and to his family for theirs

Contents

Foreword, JAN CRAIG SCRUGGS / ix

Foreword, ADRIAN CRONAUER / xiii

Introduction / xvii

Between the Lines / 1

Acknowledgments / 115

Foreword

JAN CRAIG SCRUGGS

The Wall was dedicated in 1982 after a parade down Constitution Avenue that included tens of thousands of Vietnam veterans. The National Vietnam Veterans Memorial is now known throughout the world as a special place where America remembers its veterans of a difficult war.

Between the Lines asks us to reflect on this magnificant memorial and what it has come to mean. The Wall is regularly featured on the covers of books and in movies. In places as diverse as Omaha, Tokyo, Beijing, and Oslo, the Memorial's chevron design has become as recognizable an American icon as the Statue of Liberty or the Washington Monument.

Why does this Memorial still stir emotions? Why do people leave heart-wrenching gifts and letters at The Wall? Why do visitors flock there to touch, to feel, to experience this magnificent and special place? Why, at this place, do we see grown men weep openly and embrace one another? *Between the Lines* helps to answer these questions. Its stunning photographs capture the emotion brilliantly.

I began the effort to create the Vietnam Veterans Memorial in 1979. With help from many veterans, from members of Congress, and from celebrities such as Bob Hope, we succeeded against overwhelming odds and got the Vietnam Veterans Memorial built in record time. It was important that the Memorial be a gift from the American people to honor Vietnam veterans. Tens of thousands of Americans donated more than eight million dollars to build the Memorial. But most important was that the name of each person killed or missing in Vietnam be engraved upon whatever design we selected.

After the moving dedication ceremony in 1982, many felt that the Vietnam Veterans Memorial would become just another monument in the nation's capital. I thought that The Wall would become essentially an annual gathering place for the men and women who participated in the war. We were all wrong! Today, eighteen years later, The Wall is Washington's most visited monument.

What makes this memorial different from other memorials? Scholars from prominent universities in the United States and Europe have published papers and complex theoretical treatises about the amazing power of The Wall. Their writing shares one commonality: The Wall is far more than just a monument.

Gustav Niebuhr of the *New York Times* noted a spiritual dimension when he studied how people leave personal items at The Wall, which most visitors approach with a reverential hush. As he pointed out, "Authorities on religion and culture liken this to people's behavior at sites considered holy in only a religious sense . . . such as the Western Wall in Jerusalem and the major Buddhist shrines of Asia." The spiritual dimension is explored through the medium of the camera in this volume.

Niebuhr's observation is surprising, because the Vietnam Veterans Memorial was not intended as a religious place at all. An inscription on the wall tells visitors clearly, "This Memorial honors the Men and Women of the U.S. Armed Forces who served in the Vietnam War." So how did this memorial to soldiers become a place that is more often than not likened to a religion shrine? One person told me that he views the Memorial as a curious combination of Mecca and the Western Wall. Both beckon the faithful for at least one pilgrimage during their lifetime, and at the end of the Western Wall people leave prayers in the crevices of the rocks.

The Memorial gets its power from names. The names. People who gave their lives thirty years ago breathe life into the wall. It is their memory that brings the pilgrims. Neighbors, parents, fellow soldiers come to The Wall. It seems that they are always present paying respects . . . and mourning.

Often they leave emotionally charged items. More than 40,000 items have been left there, ranging from an early 1960s television set to wedding rings, knives carried in Vietnam, beautiful flowing prose, and family albums. The act of doing so allows many to say goodbye, and to find peace. Yet not just those who know names on The Wall leave items. Americans who know none of the names leave offerings, as do visitors from all over the world.

Each year, two ceremonies are held at The Wall. On Veterans Day and Memorial Day, thousands travel from across the nation to be there. There are thoughtful speeches given. An active duty military color guard provides a traditional patriotic salute. The crowd says the Pledge of Allegiance. Yet again it is the names. The names draw the people there to show respect, for it is at The Wall that visitors commune with the spirits of the departed.

Jeffrey Ochsner, a professor of architecture at Washington University in St. Louis, has written a provocative scholarly essay in the School of Architecture's magazine. In the piece he asks, "How can its ability to touch us be understood? Will it continue to touch future generations in the same way? What will be the Memorial's significance in 100 or 200 years? Will the Memorial mean anything after several centuries have passed?" If indeed the power of The Wall is due only to the presence of living participants, will not its power diminish over time?

The author surveyed the writings of anthropologists, sociologists, psychiatrists, and other scholars. His study revealed that the power of The Wall is owing in part to its majestic setting—for both the Lincoln Memorial and the Washington Monument can be seen from The Wall. Indeed, Maya Lin incorporated both of these massive vertical structures in the design of her masterpiece.

Ochsner also pointed out quite properly that The Wall has a secret power that few have articulated. The Wall is made of a reflective polished granite. When one views a name on The Wall one also views one's self.

As he says, "It is no wonder that we find it almost impossible to leave the Vietnam Veterans Memorial. As we look into our gaze it draws us in and reaches within us. . . . Even visitors who personally knew none of the named often end up making rubbings from the wall. Or, they leave something behind, something of themselves. In either case, we can understand . . . that each of us is trying to preserve the connection we have achieved."

Because of this remarkable memorial, the Vietnam Veterans Memorial Fund has ongoing programs to help people to better understand The Wall and the veterans it honors. We have developed The Wall That Heals, a half-scale traveling replica that has been seen by hundreds of thousands on a nationwide tour. We have distributed thousands of books nationwide to high schools, telling about the Memorial and the veterans who are honored there. We have developed many important programs as we celebrate a year of activities to commemorate the Memorial through education and other efforts, and there are many more planned for the next decade.

Yes, what we are commemorating is more than just a Memorial. This graceful shrine will beckon future generations to experience its power as the veterans of Vietnam are remembered. And they, too, will be moved. As Jeffrey Ochsner points out, the experience of the Memorial, "is rare and remarkable. It is an experience that will capture those in the future as it captures us today."

Tom Morrissey is to be congratulated for his magnificent work—*Between the Lines* is a memorial in itself.

Foreword

ADRIAN CRONAUER

When someone speaks of the Vietnam Veterans Memorial, we immediately think of America's National Vietnam Veterans Memorial in Washington, D.C.; we usually call it, simply, The Wall. The United States, though, is not the only country to memorialize its sons and daughters who died in the Vietnam conflict.

In the fall of 1992, I was invited to Australia to take part in the dedication of that country's Vietnam Forces National Memorial. Among the things I learned about that wonderful land was that, in the sixties, when Aussie troops joined Americans in Vietnam, groups opposing the war were even more vocal in Australia than were their counterparts in America, and the issue was far more divisive there than here in the states.

Although the Australian Memorial is in Canberra, I spent the first six days of my trip in Sidney being interviewed by reporters from almost every medium, both print and broadcast.

One of the best of those interviews was conducted in the studios of the Australian Broadcasting Company (roughly the equivalent of America's NPR). The lady conducting the interview had done her homework and, in addition to the usual questions about the film *Good Morning Vietnam*—what was real and what was Hollywood? What is Robin Williams like? How did the film come about?—she asked many thoughtful, insightful, and sometimes hard questions about Vietnam and life for those who served there.

As I soon was to learn, though, the Australian interviewer had been one of those opposed to her country's involvement in the Vietnam conflict. Her old agenda as a war protester apparently was still on her mind because, during the interview, she astounded me by saying, "Well, I suppose by now enough time has passed that we can begin to forgive you for what you did."

My guardian angel must have whispered in my ear what to say because I never hesitated. Instantly, I replied, "I don't believe you'll find anyone who served in Vietnam who feels he needs to be forgiven for anything. On the other hand, though, you *are* correct in one respect."

"What's that?" she asked.

"I believe by now enough time has passed that we can begin to forgive you for what you did," I answered.

I have related that incident to many veterans as a way to present the idea that after all these years it finally is time for healing and forgiveness. The construction of The Wall marked the beginning of the healing time. In fact, some will say, the main idea of The Wall is healing.

Part of the healing process is letting go of our anger and frustration and hurt and pain and, instead, learning to forgive. And one way to help that process is to visit The Wall. It is always a profound and personal experience because almost everyone knows someone—a father, grandfather, an uncle, a cousin, a brother, a son, a neighbor, a classmate—whose name is written there.

Shortly after they built the original Wall, someone realized that only a minute percentage of Americans would ever get to the nation's capital to visit it. So a half-scale model of the memorial was built using lightweight panels that could be disassembled and loaded on a flatbed truck. This "Moving Wall" began touring the country. It would be taken to a community, usually at the behest of a veterans group, and set up for a week or so in a quiet grove or churchyard or park.

The response was so enthusiastic a second moving wall was built; one toured east of the Mississippi and the other in the west. Soon, a third moving wall was created to tour only on the West Coast. At this writing, there are five moving walls, each booked for at least a year or more into the future.

For years I have been traveling to veterans reunions and, frequently, these reunions include appearances of one of the moving walls. Sometimes, I go for the sole purpose of participating in a memorial service at one of them. Each time, I feel the same emotional impact, the same profound sense of awe and reverence and solemnity as I experience whenever I visit the original Wall in Washington.

And I see the faces. Each time, I see the faces of those who served and of those who lost their loved ones.

Tom Morrissey's pictures deal with these faces—the same faces I see time and again at The Wall. He shows us faces that speak to us of their personal struggles to forgive and to heal.

A few of the faces in this book I recognize. I've talked with still fewer of the people in Tom's photographs. Most, though, I don't recognize, at least in the sense that I don't know their names nor do I recall ever meeting these specific individuals. Still, in what is to me a more fascinating way, I feel I know them all because I really have seen them all at The Wall.

I've seen their eyes. Through those eyes, I believe I've seen a little of their souls. And sometimes—just sometimes—when I look at my own friend's name on The Wall, I glimpse almost the same look in my own eyes reflected from the shiny black granite surface.

As you view Tom's photographs, pay special attention to the eyes. If you served in Vietnam or if you knew someone who served there but never returned, think: have your eyes ever shown that same look in your mirror? If so, then perhaps you, knowingly or not, are part of our long national process of forgiving and healing.

Introduction

There are, at most, a handful of definitive events that forever shape the outcome of our lives. For me, the Vietnam experience was one such event; my first pilgrimage to The Wall was another. On November 11, 1983, I made my first visit to the National Vietnam Veterans Memorial in Washington, D.C. Alone, as I had arrived at my unit in Vietnam many years before, I approached the Memorial on foot from the Metro station, the November weather a bit chilled and damp, as I recall. I was wearing my flight jacket, cameras in hand, not knowing what, if anything, to expect. I crossed the heavily trafficked avenue and came upon several veterans, "out of uniform" as we often were back then, forming a ragtag-looking Veterans Day Color Guard for the now-traditional ceremonial wreath laying at the Memorial's vortex. I asked for directions to the Memorial from one of the vets who stood off to the side from the others. OD bush hat tipped high on one side, he looked to the trees, seeming to see beyond the area with the distant stare veterans of that war are known for. He answered, "There it is. Go for it, man." He shook my hand and added, "Welcome home!" The color guard began to march off in a rather loose formation as I went on. The air seemed to thicken as the somber mood of the day overcame me. Approaching from the rear, I continued on down to The Wall after taking a photo of this fellow veteran and the others who, like most I had known from the war, I would most likely never see again.

Walking past the trees on that initial visit, I encountered a mix of emotions, some of which had been locked away for more than twelve years. Suddenly, faces, names, events all began to erupt as the overall scale of the era—the war, the smells and sounds, the lives lost, the day—all came to life before me.

In the first couple of years at the Vietnam Veterans Memorial, the grassy area atop The Wall was not yet closed to visitors. My first encounter with the Memorial was from that point of view, fitting for a former helicopter pilot, an aerial view looking down upon the troops below. At that moment, I made the personal commitment to capture the stories on film, to document the healing process, to put my own spirits to rest, to offer commemoration to those names on The Wall, my friends, relatives, comrades, classmates, my fellow soldiers.

Now, looking back over the thirty years since Vietnam, much has unveiled itself to me through my quest for resolution of the foremost life-changing event in my life. Vietnam found me, a twenty-year-old aeronautical science student, volunteering for U.S. Army Warrant Officer Flight Training along with my good and closest friend from high school, Lance Lofman. Lance received fixed-wing training; he was an Otter pilot and he had it made. Lance was killed within two months of his arrival "in country." I, by the grace of God, survived unscathed, and his memory has never left my side.

My goal in 1969, to fly professionally for the airlines after the war, was cut short by an overstock of pilots, many of whom would soon be furloughed in those recession years of the early 1970s. After my release from active duty, I was number 600 or so on a waiting list for an aviation slot in the reserves in southern Florida. I returned to college to study political science, then photography, later turning to sculpture, creating forms that somehow looked similar to burned-out, twisted fragments of steel, perhaps mental images of blown bridges, spent aircraft—who knows?

My combat decorations—awarded for what? Perhaps for safely executing an emergency landing from low altitude of an incapacitated, fully loaded aircraft in three feet of water in a rice paddy with no casualties (an event that was reported in an issue of *1st Aviation Brigade Magazine*), perhaps for covering a late-night medevac from a fire support base after a rocket attack—Firefly pilot of the "light-ship"—later that night capturing a VC suspect in the vicinity. Perhaps for the months of flying night missions along the Ho-Chi-Minh Trail, a 50-cal. mounted in one door, a mini in the other. Perhaps for flying CAs with the

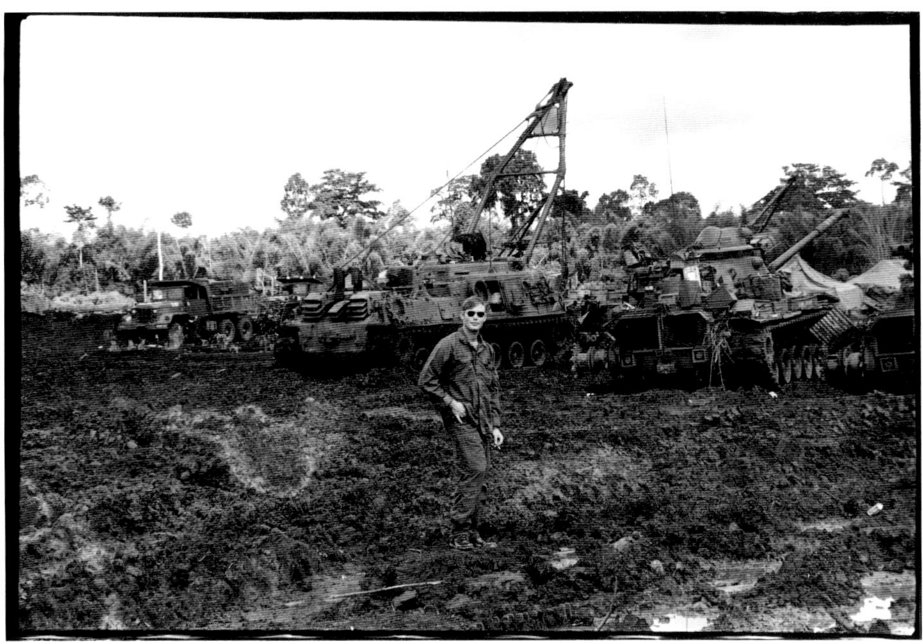

Vietnam, 1970

Special Forces or Navy Seals. I was an AC they liked to fly with, requested by name. AFVN beating Jimi Hendrix or the Stones in one ear, company Fox Mike blaring in the other; "Off Guard," someone would blurt out on 125.5 VHF, the open frequency reserved for emergencies. I was "Warlord 23," Little Annie Fanny or the Pink Panther proudly painted on the fiberglass avionics hatch nose cover of my UH1H, "Huey." Cabin doors long removed, the cool breeze brushing across my face as we skated barely above the treetops at one hundred knots.

And the fond memories? I have those to share as well. Once, on a mission, my door gunner, Spc. 4 Jinks, felt a stinging in his boot, only to discover a 7.62 round lodged between his toes. Later, upon post-flight inspection, we would discover several other rounds sunk into the fuselage and main rotors. Or the time I glanced to see Johnson, my crew chief, standing outside the aircraft on the skids, 1500 feet in the air, asking if I wanted the windshield cleaned. Could I forget CW2 Deedy and his famed armored seat protector with the shining fifty-caliber enemy round penetrating it, stopping only inches from his flesh; the much sought-after missions to pick up steaks for company parties or to make last-minute beer runs to a unit standing down at some set of coordinates?

But the names are inscribed on The Wall, all in a row, names of entire flight crews who went down together. Names I know. Eight panels on The Wall, or is it ten, attest to the sacrifice made that year. They can never be forgotten. For me, combat decorations were unimportant, as to many of us during that unpopular period of the war; we never wanted them, didn't think to even ask for them. They were for the lifers! I was "short"; that was all that mattered! It was 1971; who was even keeping track anymore? By March, I was training a VNAF copilot, POL was few and far between as airfields across Vietnam closed down. Vietnamization was in full gear. The war, winding down, a few more flings into the "Cambode" around the Parrot's Beak, "thirty days and a wake-up." I was out-of-there! Memories and decorations were soon to be put aside with that old uniform where no person would even know to ask. I was barely a young man, in the middle of something unlike anything I had known before, far away from home, family, friends, football, my life in "the world."

"The world!" My first day back, I was being refused service for a beer in the San Francisco International Airport because I didn't have a valid driver's license. Twenty-three years of age, warrant officer bars, aviator wings, two rows of ribbons. A Vietnam stare easily over a mile long. DD214 in my hand, and still no beer. Being discharged only hours before, my military ID had been surrendered at the out-processing center where, after a brief physical, I had been served the "welcome home" steak and fries, complete with bottomless cup of coffee, and sent on my way. I flew home to Florida that night; the next evening I walked my mother's dog. That first night back—"the world!"—nothing had changed; everything remained the same. "Had I been away?" a neighbor asked earlier that day.

We veterans, and those closely associated with us, all have similar stories, similar memories, similar feelings. They had been held inside until, well over a decade later, we were able to come together in numbers. People we could talk to, finally, in a way "standing down," removing our uniforms and with them the years of internalized emotions both good and bad, ultimately putting closure to this life-changing experience that left so many casualties, so many wounded, so many suffering over the loved ones they lost. Had it been another war, as David Bowie later sang, "We could be heroes."

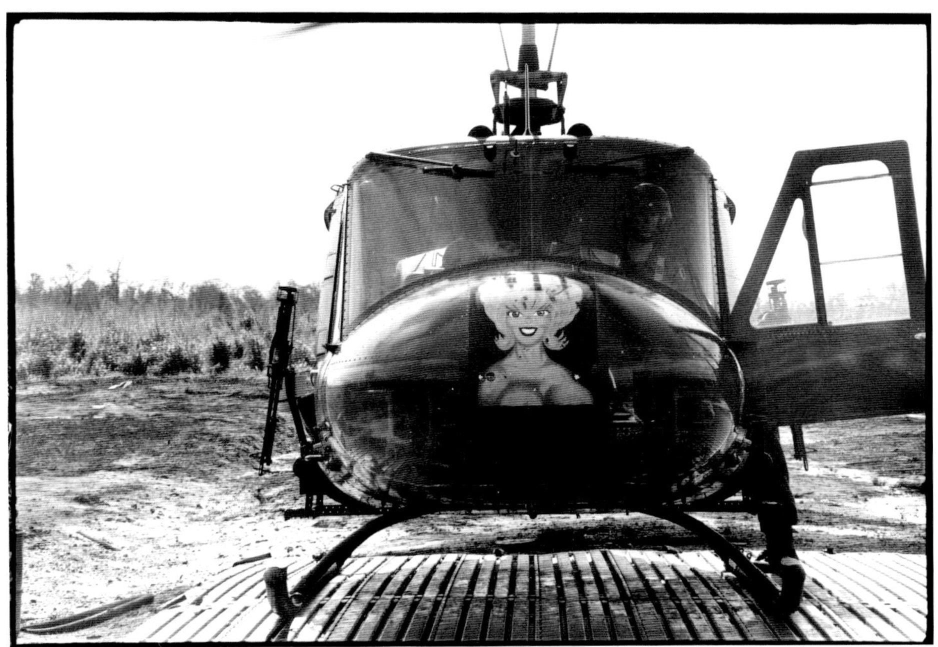

Vietnam, 1971

Many of us have been fortunate in Vietnam's aftermath, many have not. For me, the Vietnam experience has unfolded as a positive one; I could not have let it be any other way. I have developed a maturity, a sense of awareness, leadership skills, and perspective that come, I believe, solely with the deep-rooted experiences, rights of passage, that only a war can bring. Only those who exper-ience it can understand or explain. We justifiably mourn our fallen comrades, some with unseen emotional scars. Veterans, for the most part, have assimilated well with our nonveteran peers, meeting success in business, in the arts, as members of the House and Senate, holding the highest offices in the nation. As well, there are large numbers of men and women who are still in need of healing the scars, amputations, irreversible wounds of battle. At times it is hard to communicate to nonvets the level one reaches in that intense situation. These attributes are not gained, as some may suggest, at paint-ball camp, where nothing is at risk, attended by mid-management executives and CEOs. How many could know, without having been there, what it means to put yourself on the line for others, maybe daily, regardless of what neighborhood they came from, to pull them from a hot LZ, to patch their wounds if there is time, to experience such adrenaline, such highs, such lows, such in-betweens, your life in the balance?

The years following that first pilgrimage to The Wall have brought with them involvement and interaction with several individuals, veterans groups, and organizations: Vietnam Veterans of America, the Vietnam Veterans Helicopter Pilot Association, the Vietnam Veterans Memorial Fund, Friends of the Vietnam Memorial, the Vietnam Veterans Institute, Veterans Leadership Program, Gold Star Mothers, the Rhode Island Vietnam Monument Committee. My visits to The Wall have led me to meet and know the women and men who served in combat as nurses, as soldiers, as Red Cross volunteers, as doctors, as our commanding general, as combat photographers, as AFVN radio personalities, as POWs. I have met mothers, wives, sons and daughters, grandchildren of veterans. I have met and known Vietnamese and Southeast Asian refugees: a Vietnamese woman who had been burned with napalm as a child, an air force colonel who had spent too many years in the Hanoi Hilton, a naval admiral whose son died from Agent Orange, the young woman who designed the black granite wall, the visionary who conceived its birth. I have met so many, many more. And those whose names are inscribed on that wall—those who laid down their lives for us who have survived and returned to continue their memory—I have met them, too.

I have also grown to recognize the pain my mother must have felt the day she brought me, her only child, to Miami International Airport to leave for that trip across the Pacific. It was another one of those moments furnished by God to help us through the day. My neighbor and high school classmate, Jerry Woods, Sgt. Woods by then, at the airport, visiting home shortly after his second tour in Vietnam, serendipitously happened by us in the terminal only to point out that I had forgotten to place about half of the brass regalia on my uniform. A bit of lightheartedness added to the heartfelt good-byes. Had I been preoccupied that morning to leave my uniform in such disarray? It was a much-needed relief from the pain that I now realize my mother must have been feeling as she left the airport alone that day, not knowing when she might see me again.

The years have also led me to meet several of my former enemy. I returned to Vietnam in 1992, alone, just as I had arrived some twenty-two years earlier, alone as I have traveled to the Memorial so many times. Vietnam, a trip that many veterans I meet say they would never make. I was at that same airport, this time passing rows and rows of discarded UH1 helicopters aligned at the side of the runway as we landed. I was armed with my camera and a mind full of questions still unanswered. I experienced the tunnels at Cu Chi. I saw, looming in the distance, Nui Ba Dinh, the Black Virgin Mountain, upon whose peak I landed countless times. I visited the Memorial Military Cemetery at Tay Ninh. I enjoyed an almost-cold Bia-Ba Muoi Ba "33 beer," co dah (with ice) atop the Rang Dong Hotel, overlooking the city and the reaches of space beyond. My last night "in country." I, with my newly introduced counterparts, former VC, NVA, ARVN, the widow of a former VNAF pilot who died in reeducation camp, a former VNAF colonel and his family waiting to leave for the United States through Thailand under the U.S. Government's Displaced Persons Program, all meeting at a restaurant in what had previously been known as Saigon. We had all been there to "fight for Vietnam," I offered in a toast. "We had just been on opposing sides of the deadly teams," leaving millions dead in the wake. A moment of silence was offered, the air seemed to thicken. The pain recalled as those from a country so long divided tried to bury their histories together and move on with their lives. As former combatants, we offered one another no regrets or guilt, only mutual respect to fallen comrades-in-arms.

War is, by definition, a deplorable set of circumstances, bringing out "the best in good men, the worst from bad," it has been written. In Vietnam, you never knew who was truly on your side. I thought briefly of the company commander I had known who put his personal advancement over the well-being of his troops. It seems I have witnessed it all. Then, as now when I am at The Wall, I had the sense that we are all somehow cast members from a play, gathering on closing night, all reviewing our roles, pondering our scripts, several cast members missing that final curtain.

I began photographing the Memorial in 1983. As with my first encounter with that black granite wall, I didn't know what to expect. I left there that first day after shooting some fifteen rolls of film, knowing I would always return. The project evolved, providing its own direction. The title, *Between the Lines: Photographs from the National Vietnam Veterans Memorial,* came to me while I was reviewing the letters home I had written from Vietnam. "Free" was scribbled in the corners of the envelopes where stamps should have been, APO address in the upper left. But reading these letters made me realize that, even with these

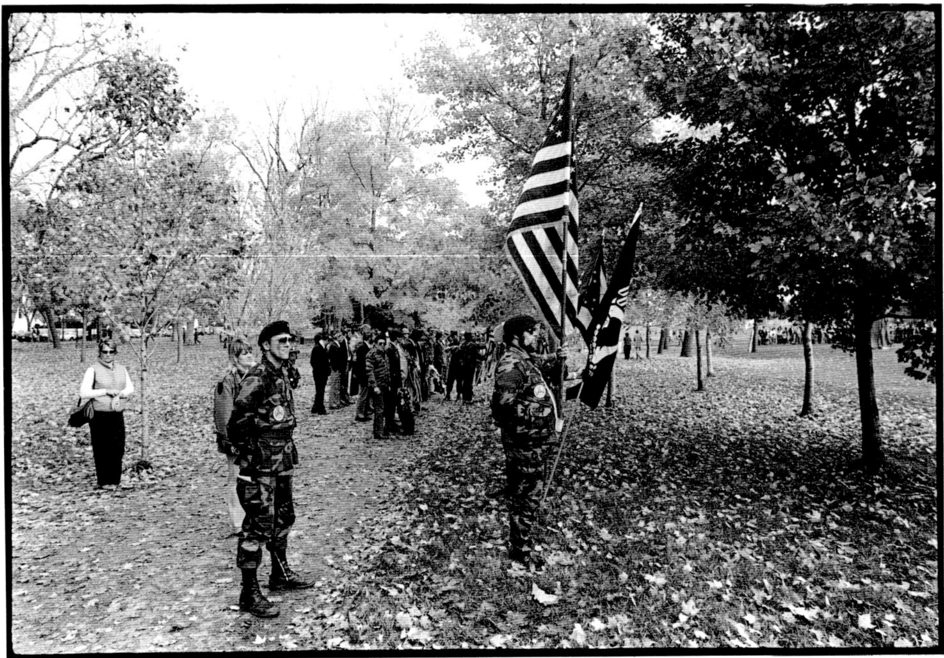

The Wall, 1983

encryptions, my family still didn't "know" Vietnam. I knew that to do that, they would need to read "between the lines." I immediately thought how, at the Memorial, we experience the same phenomenon, seeing our reflections, our lost spirits shine from the glossy black surface that exists between the lines of names, listed in chronological order of death.

With this body of photographic work, my intent is to capture the healing process that I and every one of us who has been associated with Vietnam have shared as a result of paying homage to our fallen comrades at the most visited memorial in our nation's history. The book is presented as a mantra, a prayer book of sorts, a connection to the process that has helped let us lay this traumatic chapter in our nation's life to rest. As I have returned year after year, I have felt a new energy coming from the black granite slab that reflects our emotions so well. The air surrounding the Memorial, thick with pain and searching in the early years, is now much lighter and reflective of sharing and joy. We who have made the journey in previous years are there to provide support for those still gathering the courage to come and lay their spirits to rest for the first time.

In my research for this book, I have crossed paths with many of the major figures of the time: American and Vietnamese leaders, admirals, commanders, and generals, the former head of the CIA, an infamous researcher of Pentagon Papers, members of the media, our commanding general, his wife, their grandchildren, former POWs—all providing thought that was the impetus for this book. All receive my deepest respect in these years following the end of America's involvement. I visited the National Park Service/MARS archives facility in Maryland, reading through the hundreds of pages of messages left at the Memorial. Several of these passages, encapsulated throughout this book of photographs, punctuate the images. The messages, like the images, are not in chronological order, but are arranged by content. They provide a needed pacing for the viewer, creating pauses in which to contemplate the images. Through *Between the Lines,* there is an opportunity to revisit The Wall, an experience that many have drawn upon over the years. The images, arranged visually, establish a rhythm that reflects the process of healing. Interlaced throughout the images are the meditations, left anonymously at The Wall, by those seeking its refuge. They are untitled but dated, not for documentation so much as to provide a sense of time. The dates, names, definitions, and explanations of the images and text are irrelevant. The images and accompanying text will speak to us clearly, bringing the healing, restorative process home to our hearts.

With this book I offer a "Welcome home!" to all.

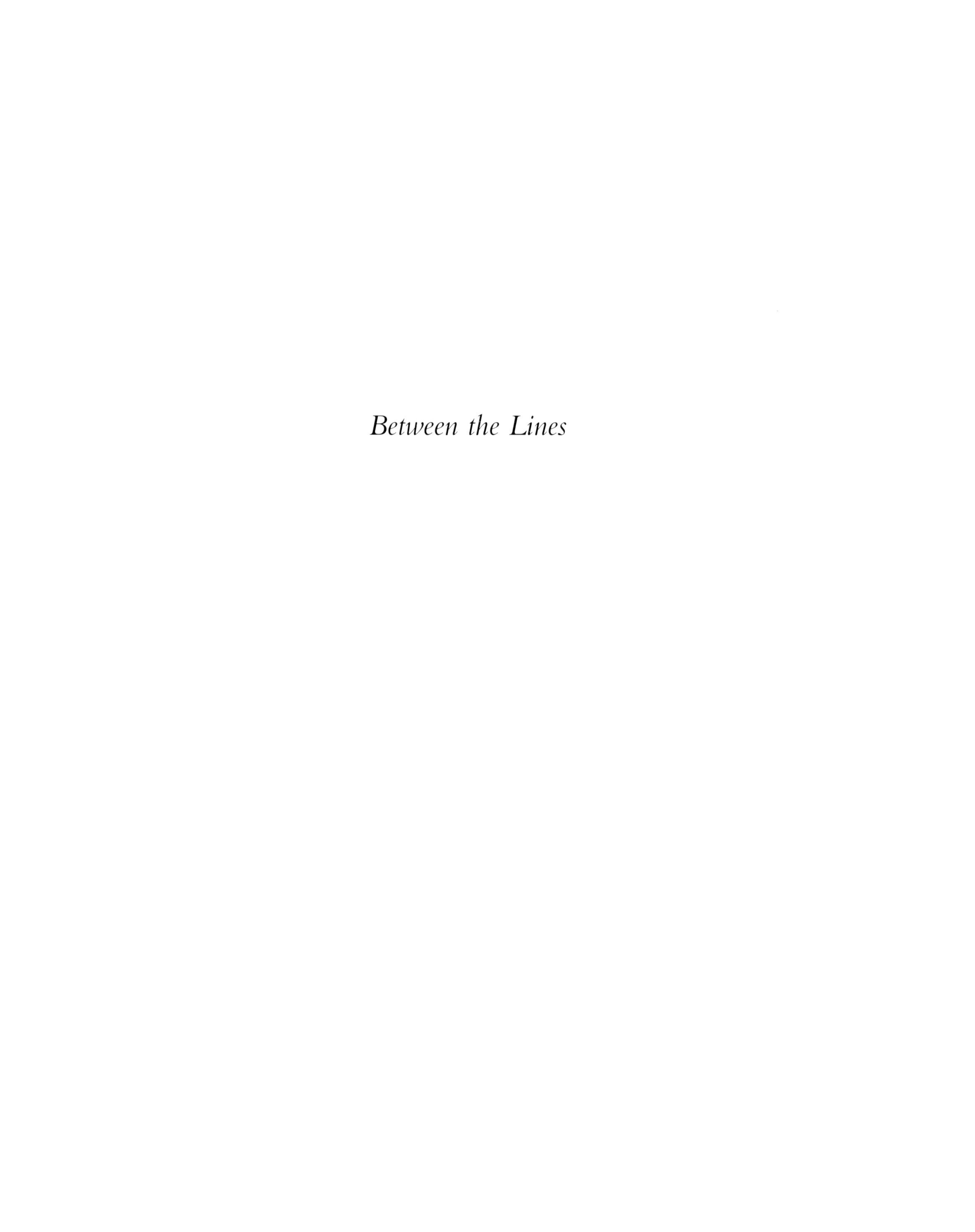

Between the Lines

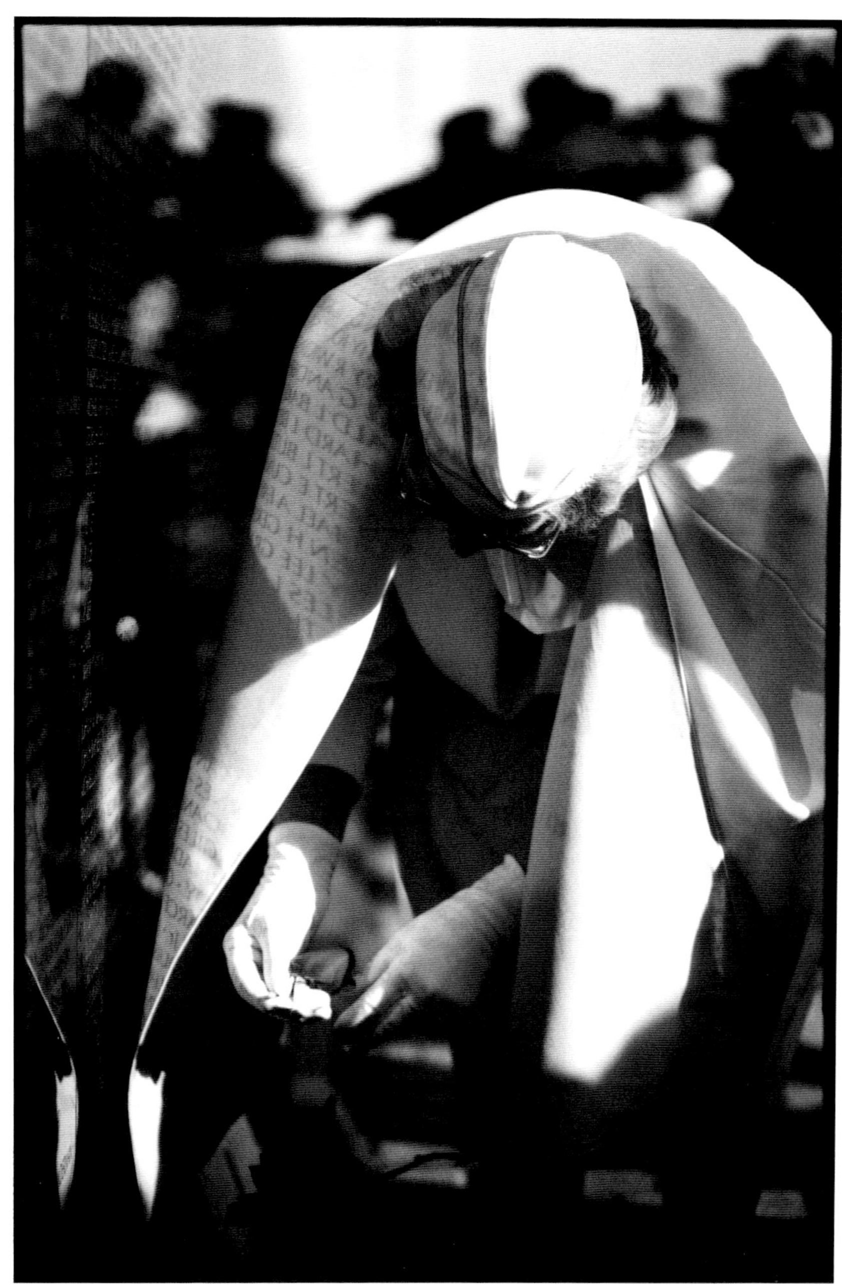

PLATE 1
1990

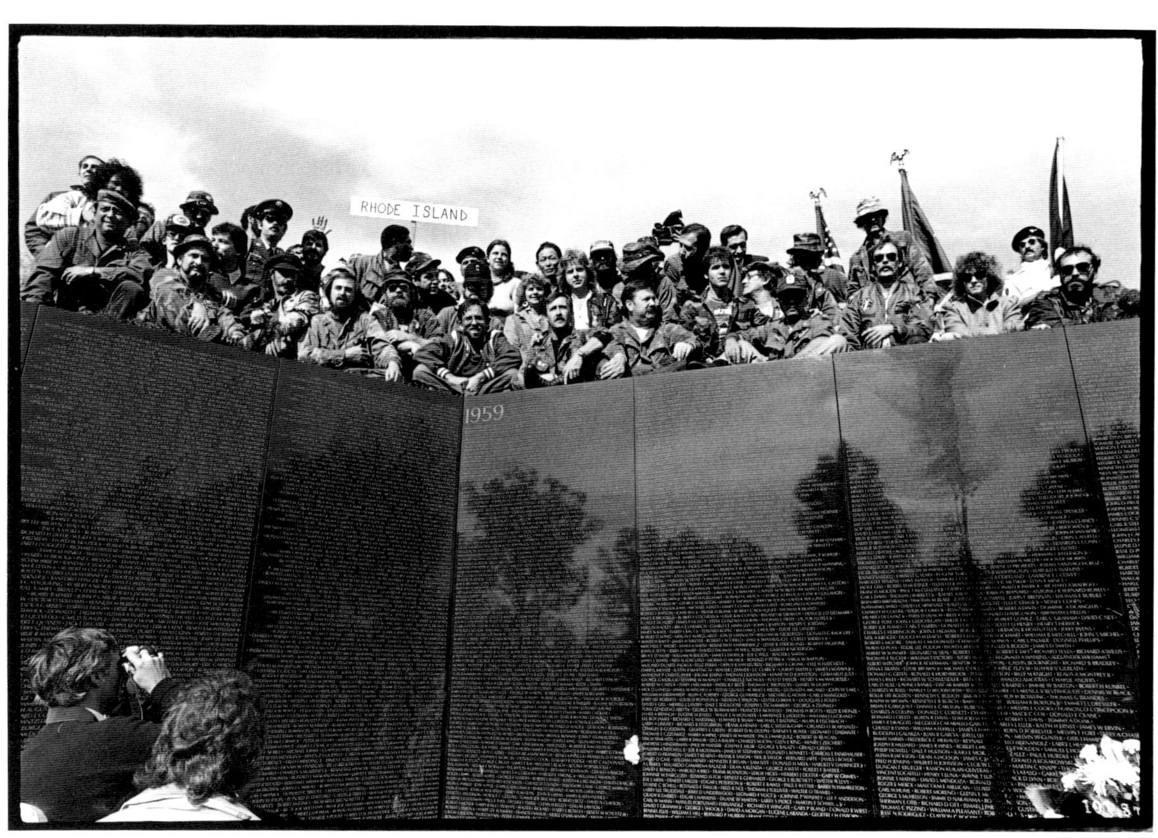

PLATE 2
1984

U.S.NAVY
1954-1975
VIETNAM
POW★MIA
YOU ARE NOT FORGOTTEN
ENLISTED MESS OPEN
SUBIC BAY R.P.

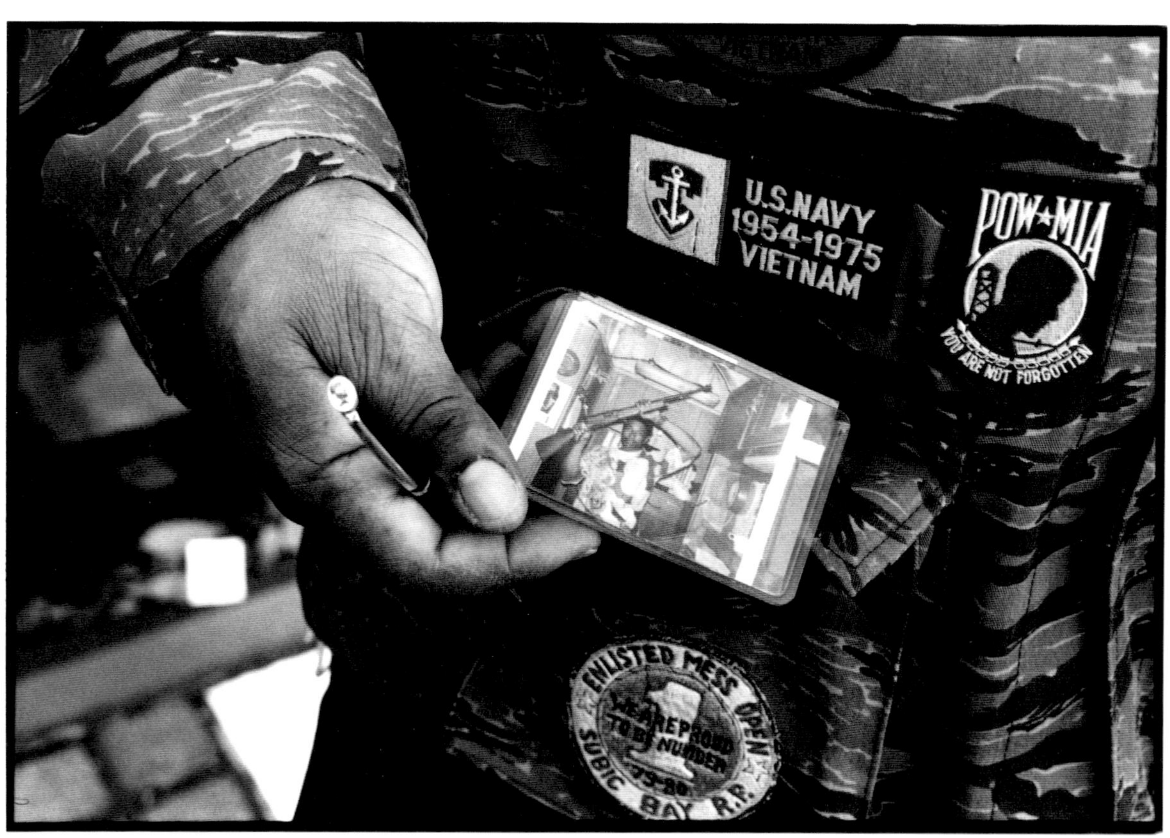

PLATE 3

1997

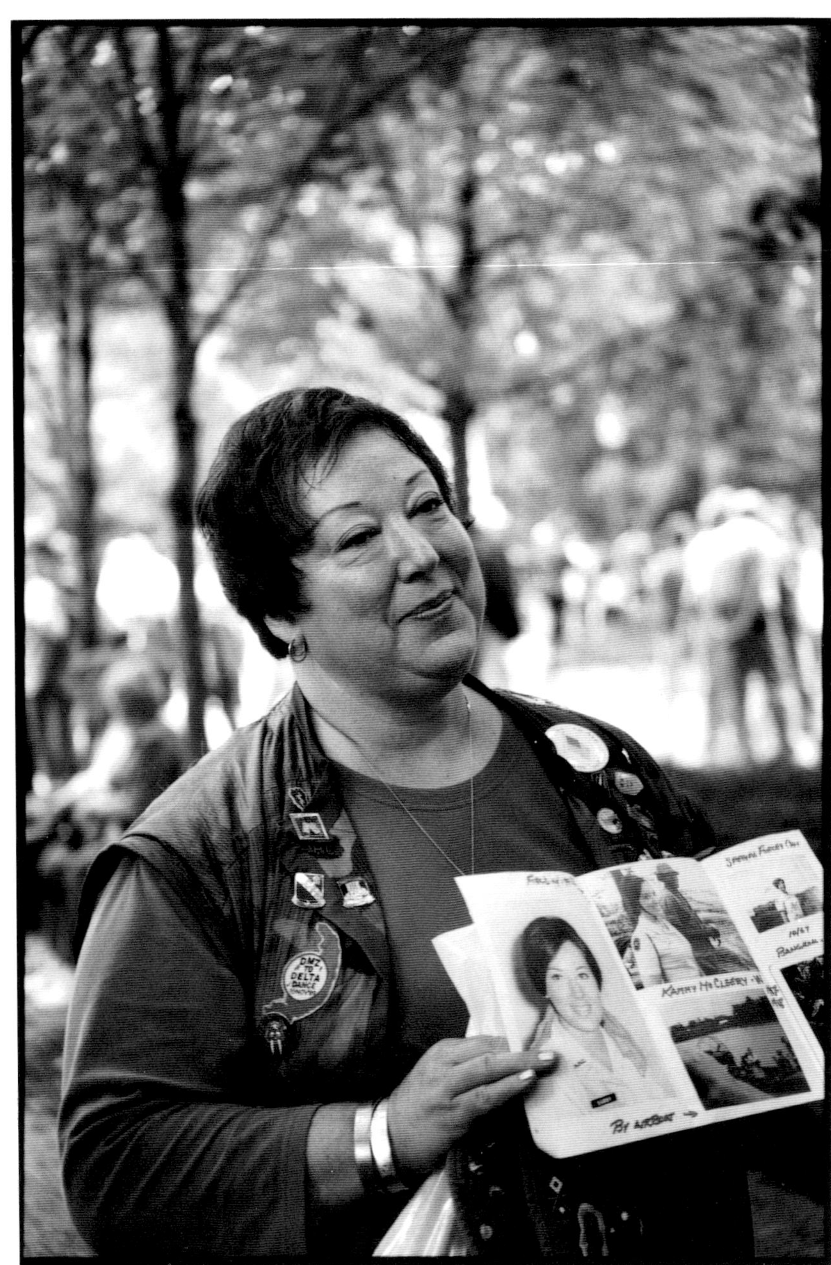

PLATE 4

1996

To Jim,

You know I never knew how much you meant to me until you were gone from me and our family. But for the last 15 years you have been on my mind so many, many times. I wish so many times you could have been here in person to experience life with us. I am reminded so often about you, through your son Jeff. I wish, so badly you could see him and be with him, and be able to talk to him and encourage him. You would be so proud of him. He is so handsome, kind and considerate. He reminds me of you in so many ways—especially his smile. I remember when you smiled (which was most of the time) your whole face light up—Jeff's does the same way. He even has a lot of your "famous" sense of humor when you get him going. I guess sometimes I get mad that you aren't here. I know it wasn't your choice to die and it wasn't God's choice for you to die. I also know how it feels to be the person left behind. I do feel thankful to have this opportunity to write these feelings to you. I know I will have these feelings about you forever and I never have to erase them from my mind. I miss you very, very much and I know I always will.

Love, Gail
June 11, 1984

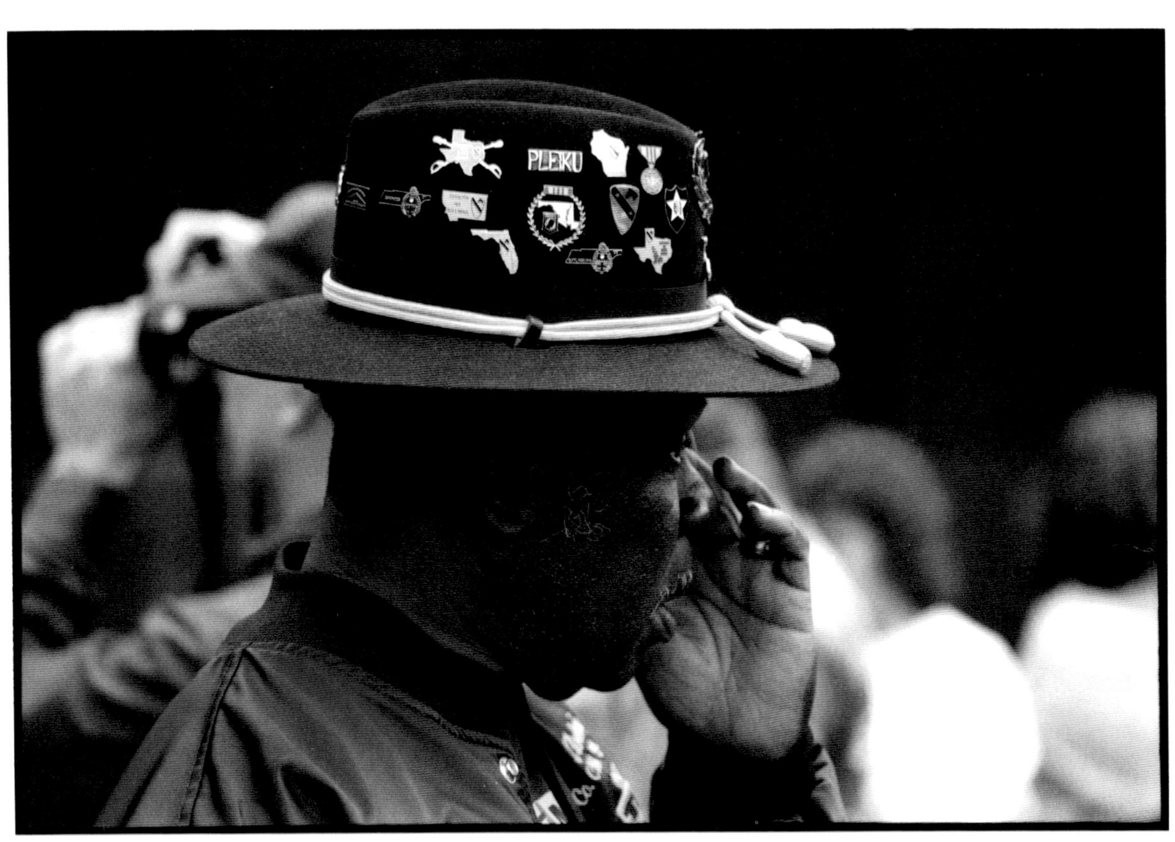

PLATE 5
1987

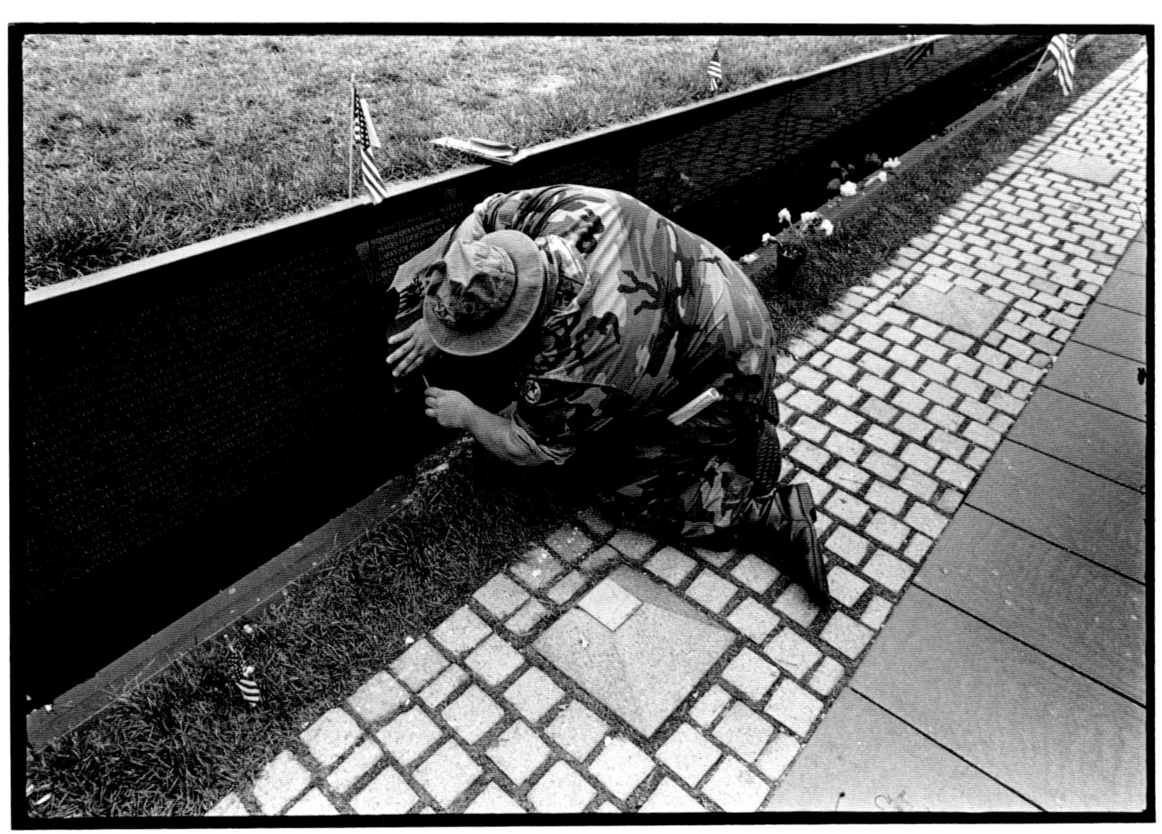

PLATE 6

1983

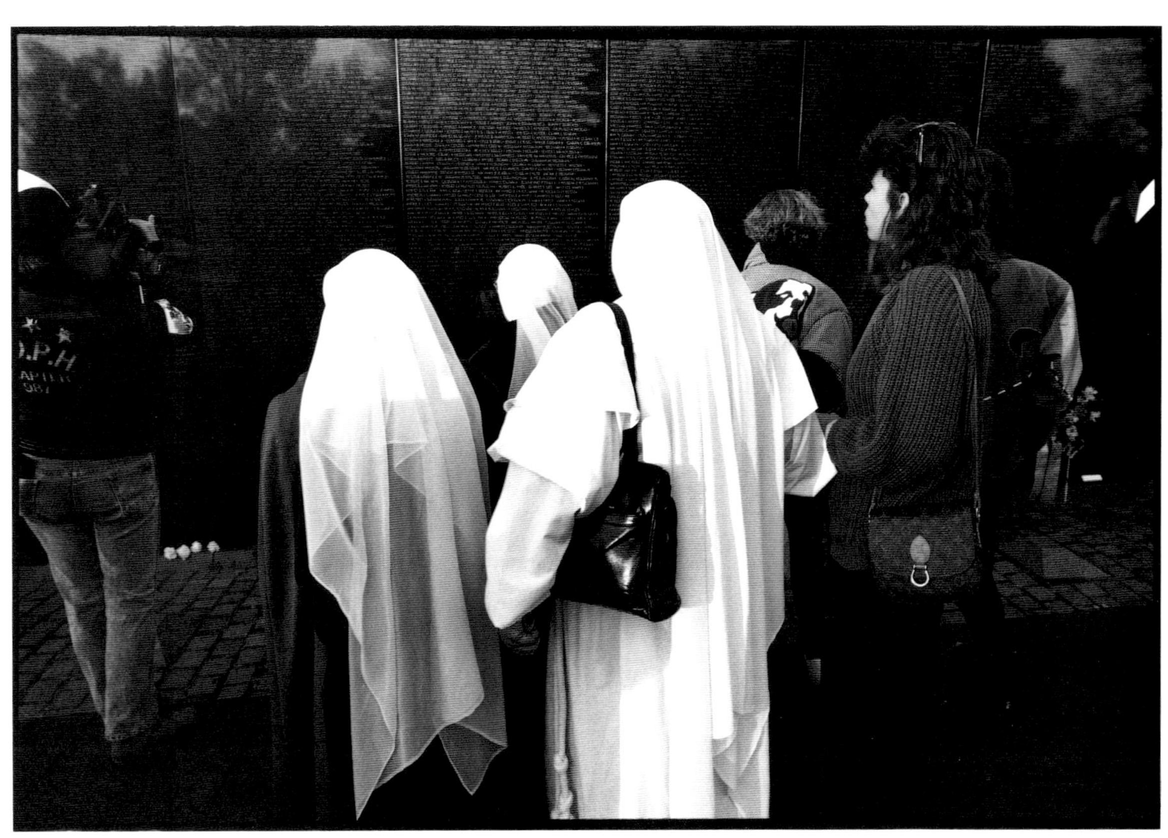

PLATE 7
1993

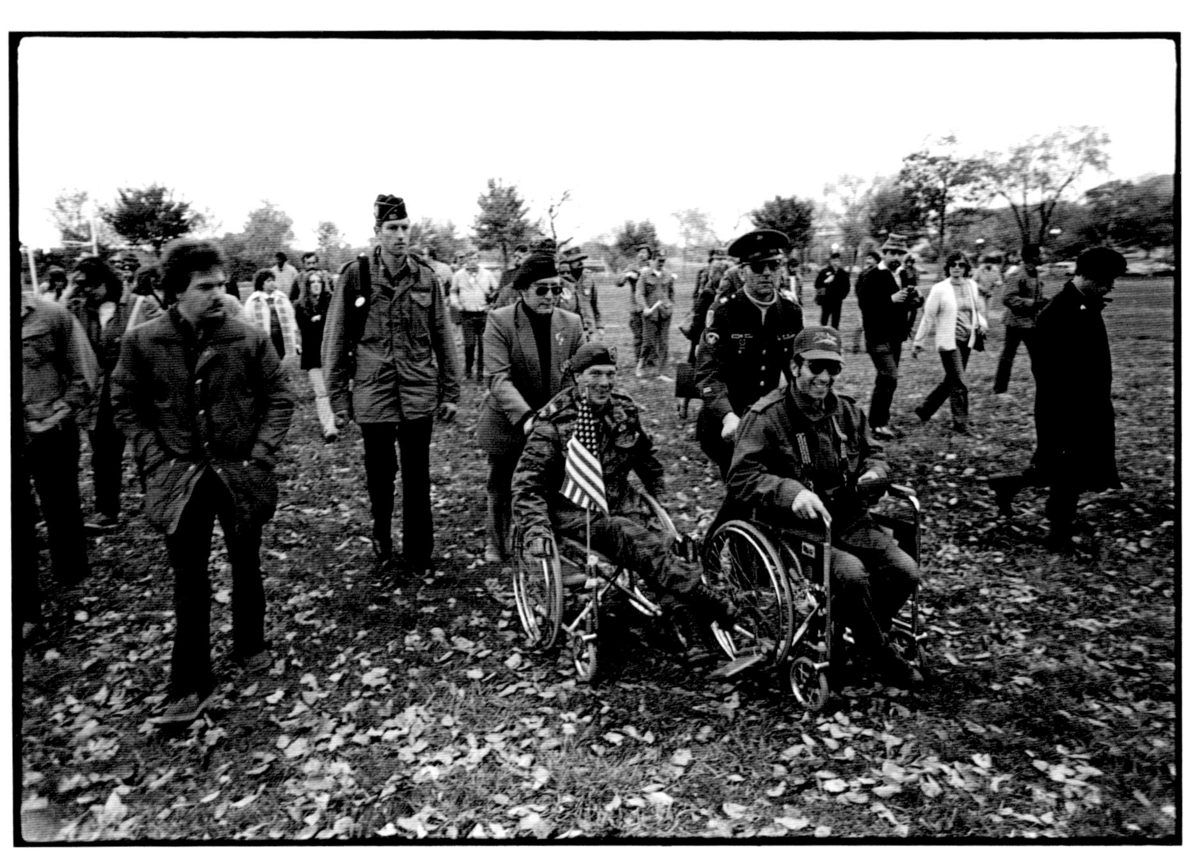

PLATE 8

1985

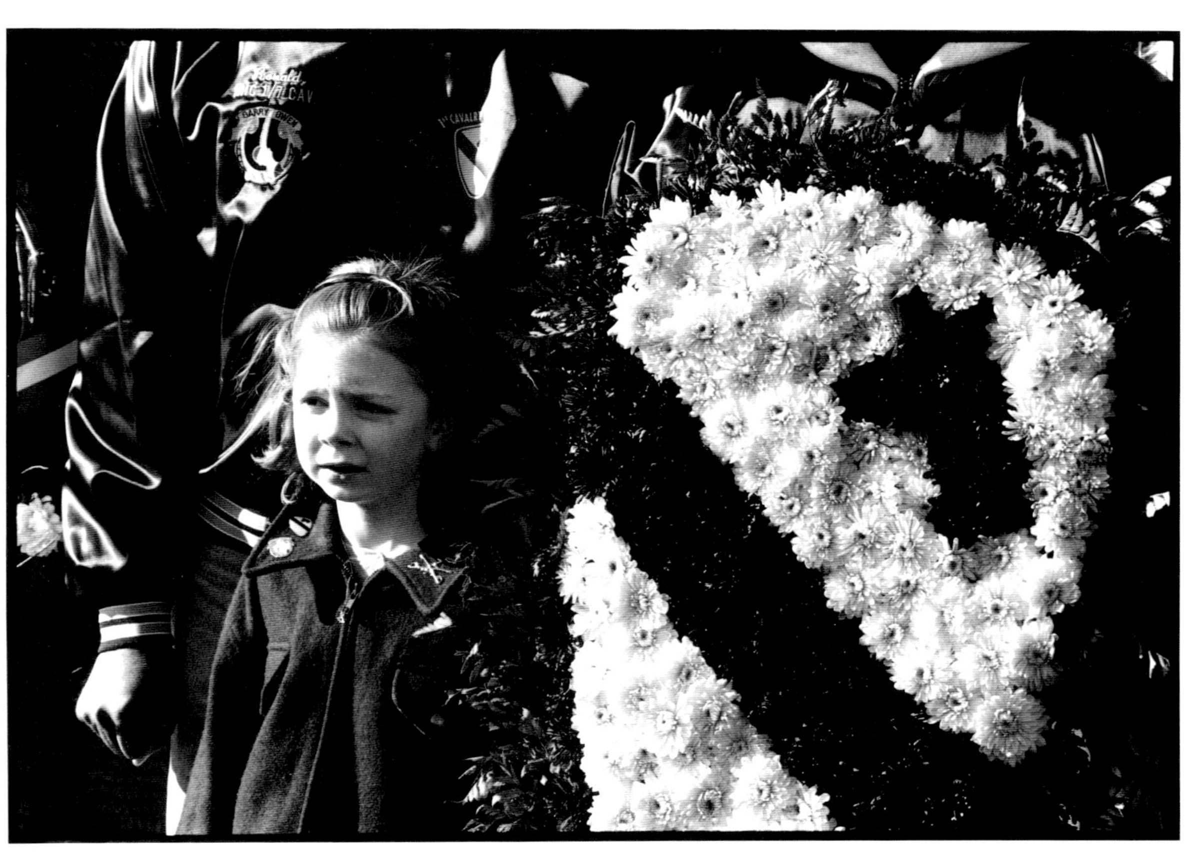

PLATE 9

1994

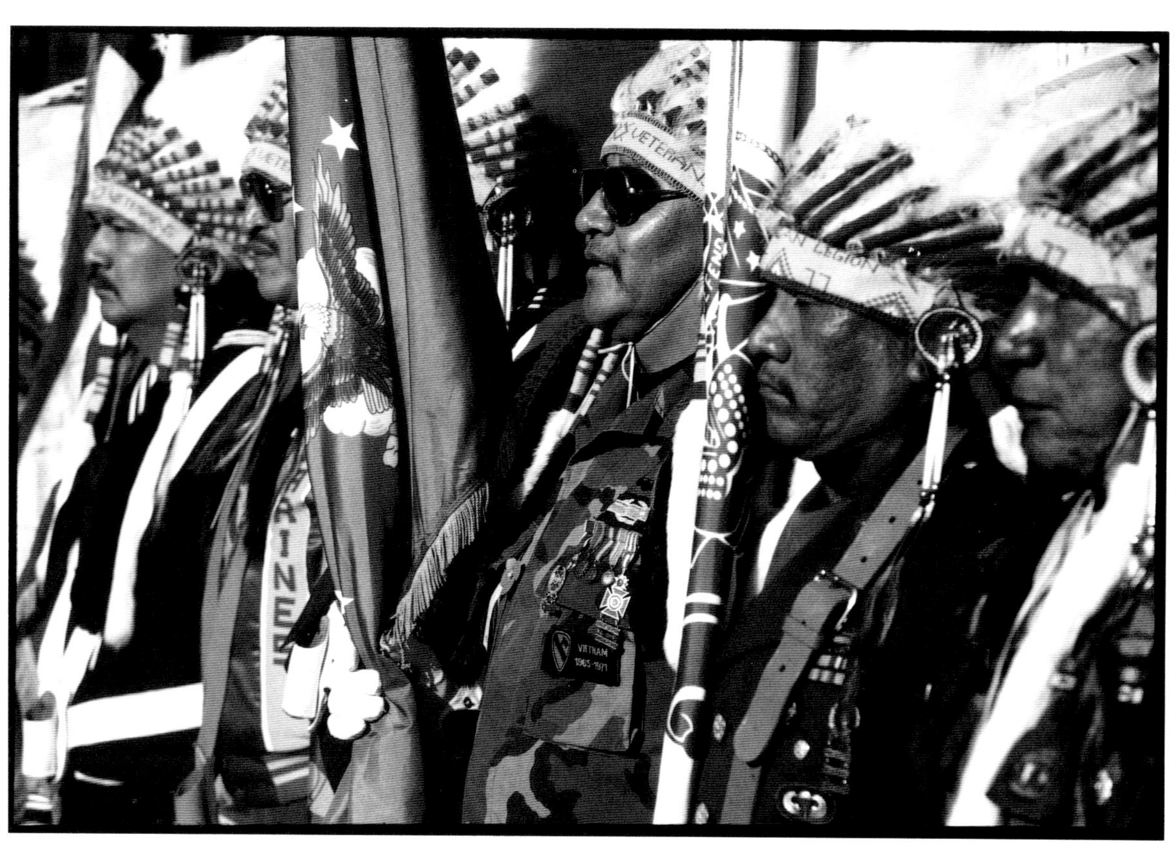

PLATE 10

1992

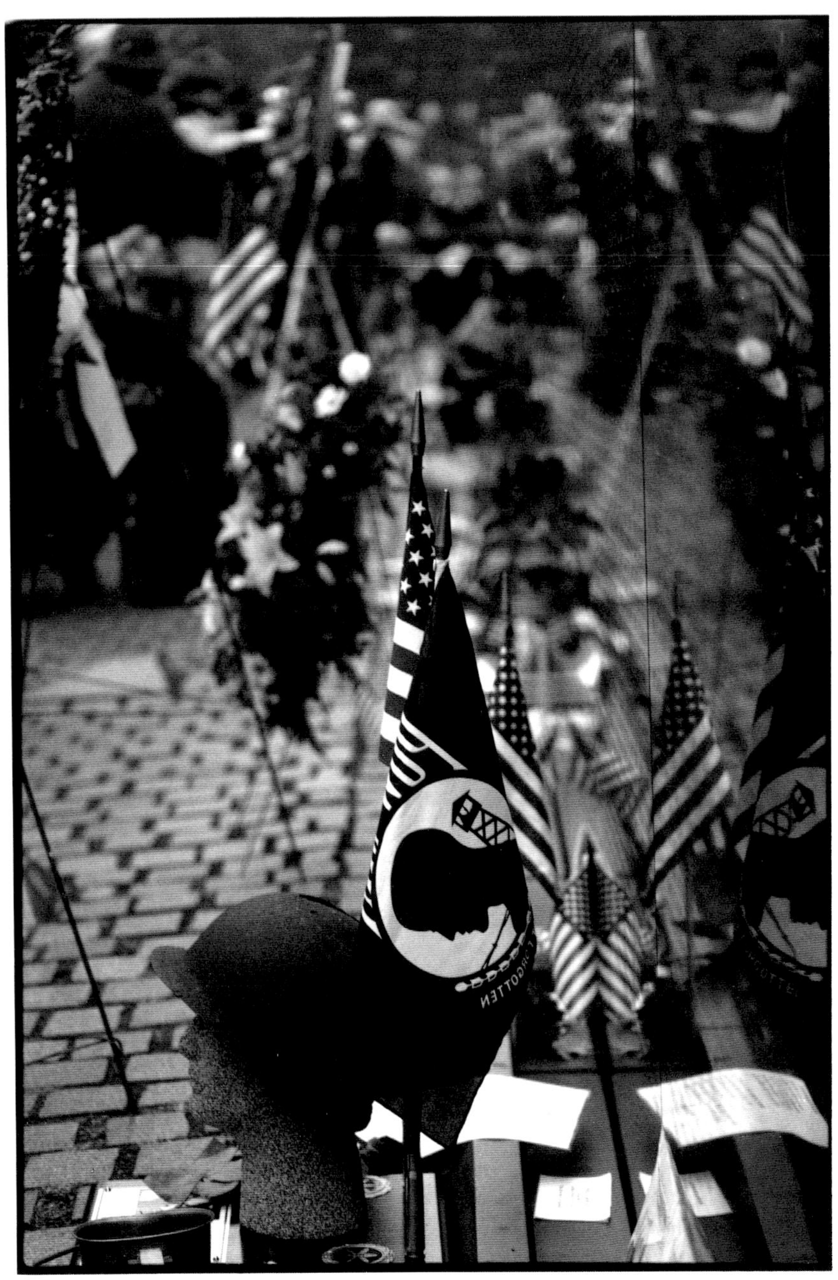

PLATE 11
1999

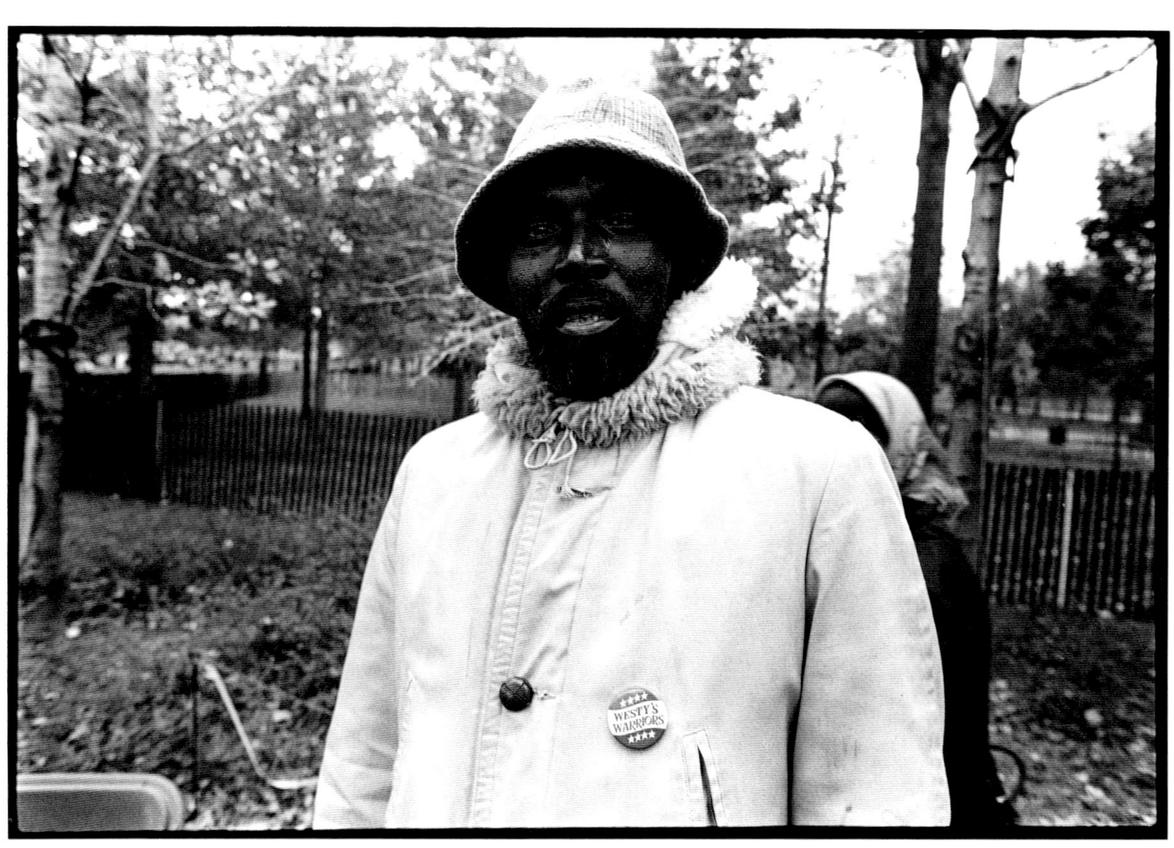

PLATE 12
1986

Together we were child warriors.
Today I'm an old man with tears for after 20 years I can say
"Good bye Brother." I love you well.

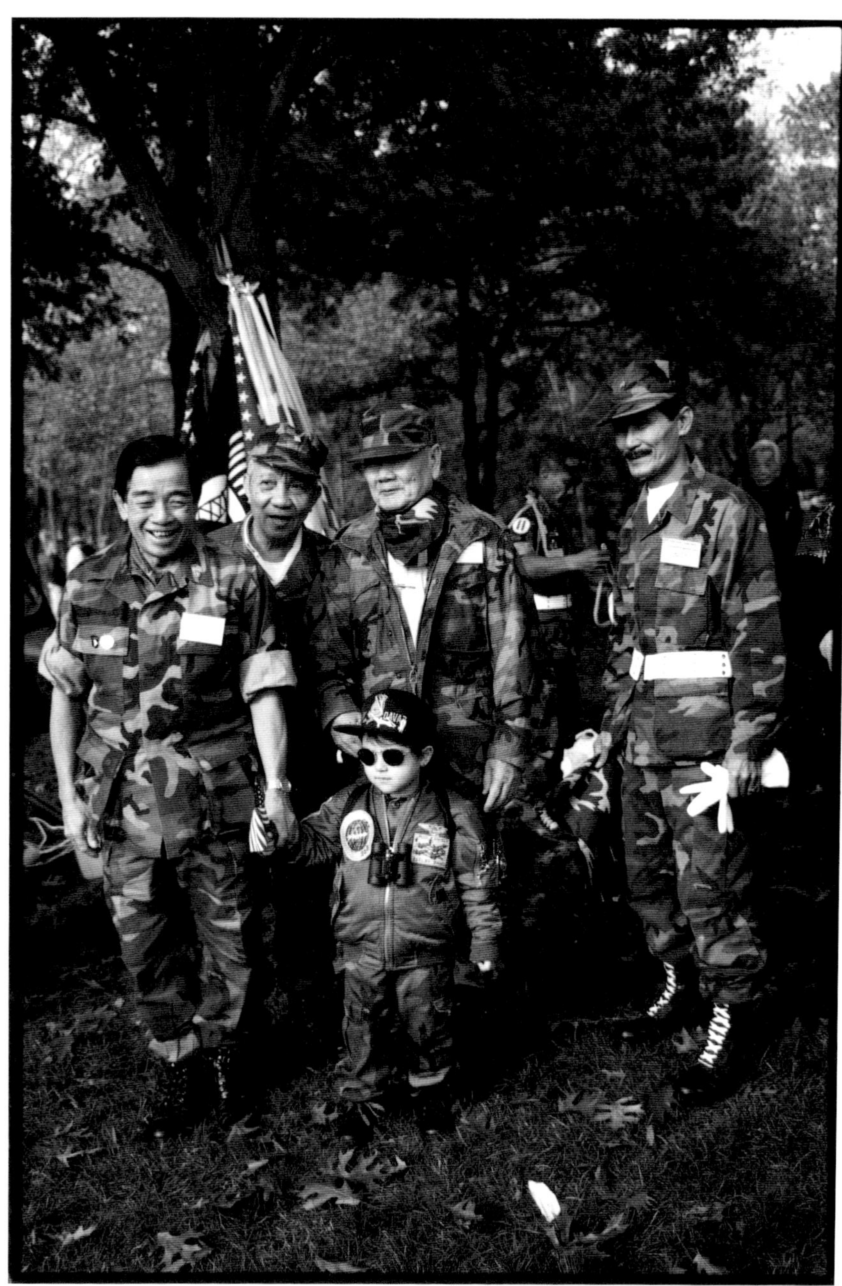

PLATE 13

1997

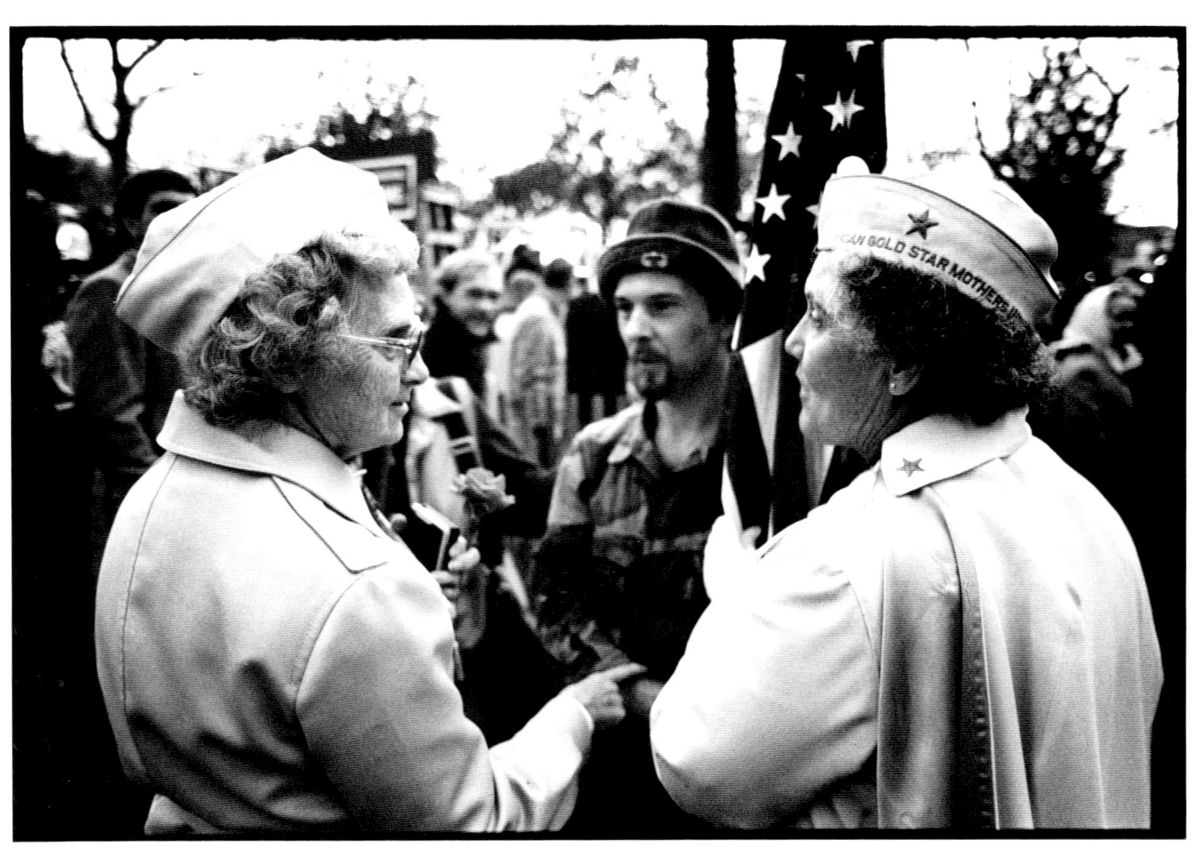

PLATE 14

1983

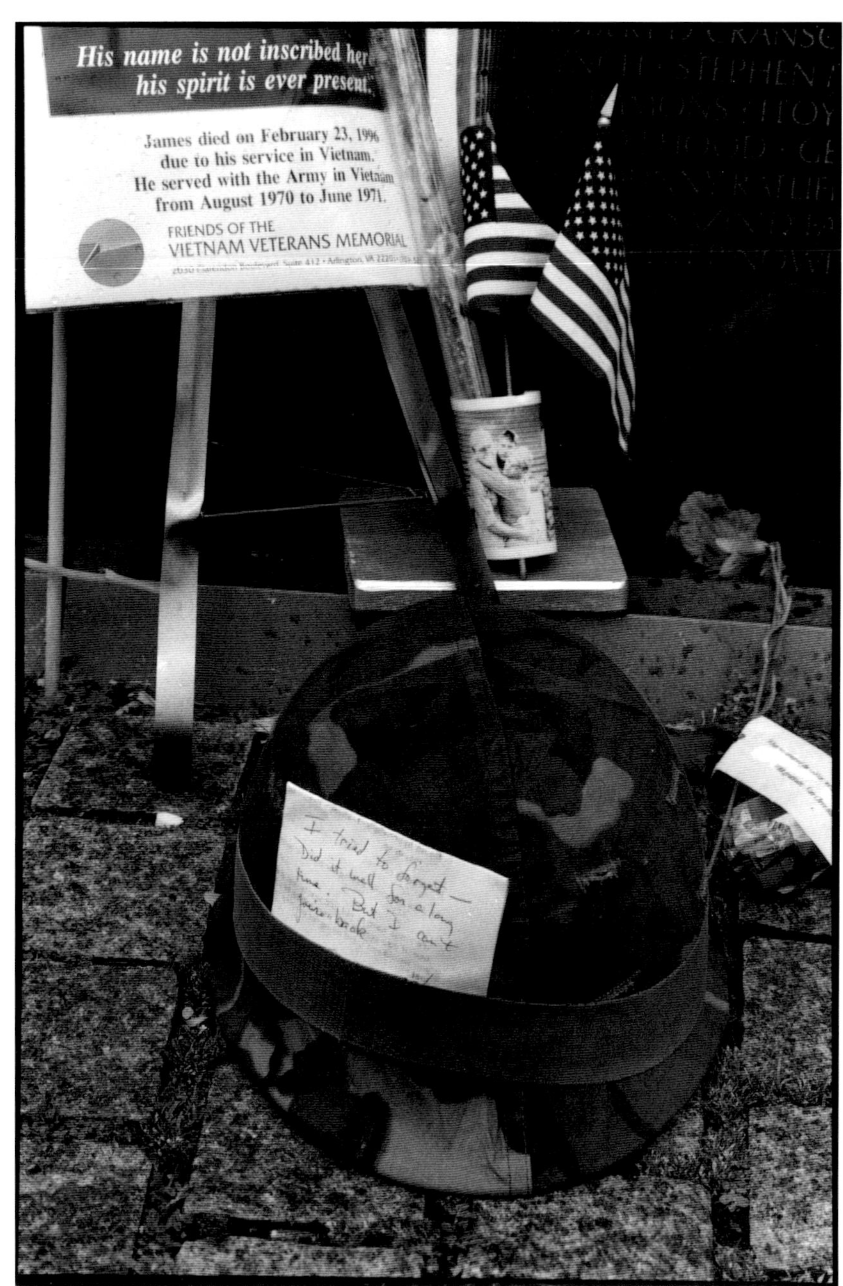

PLATE 15
1997

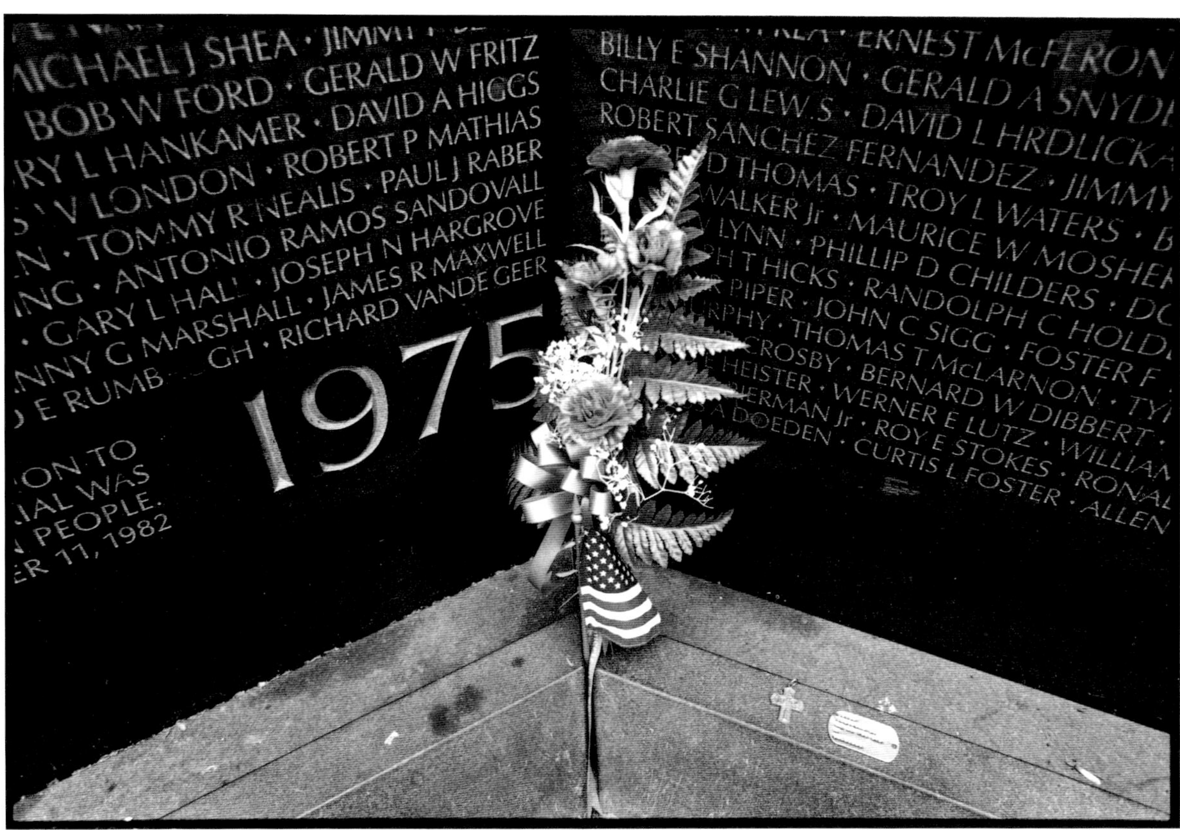

PLATE 16

1991

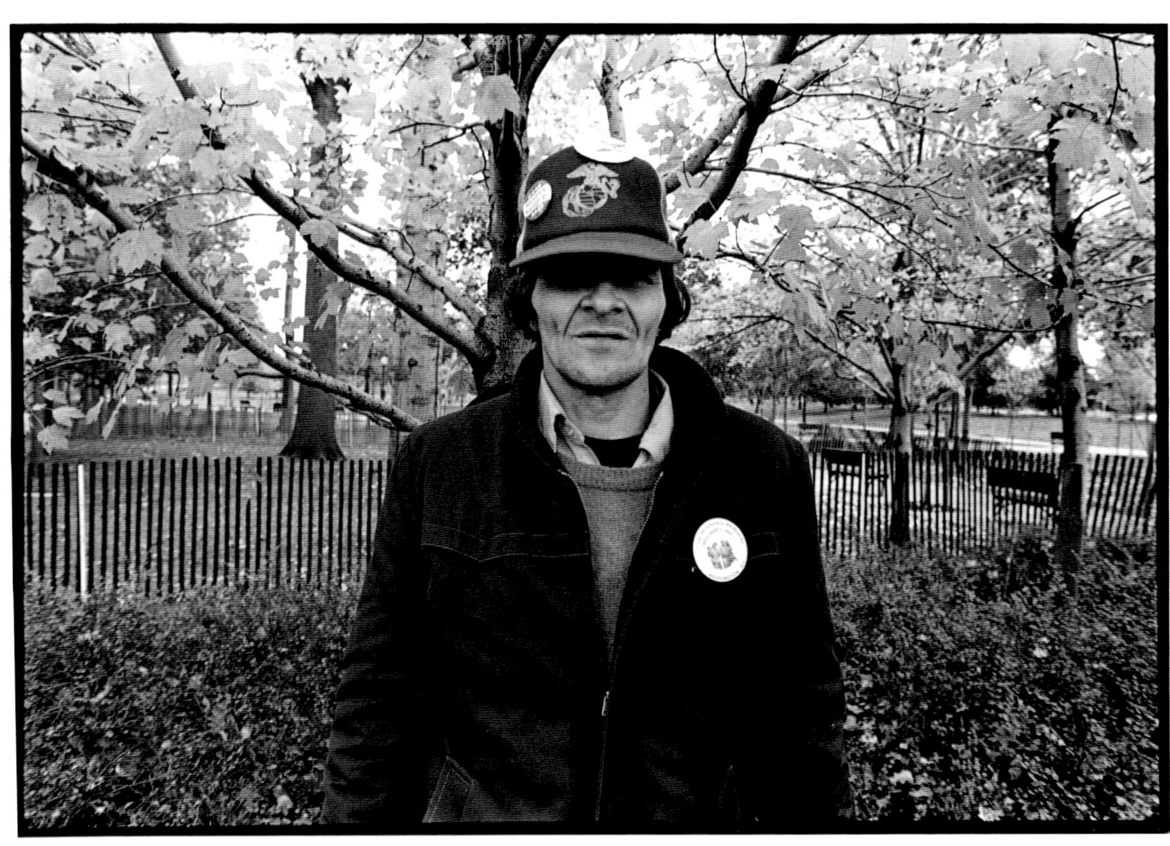

PLATE 17
1986

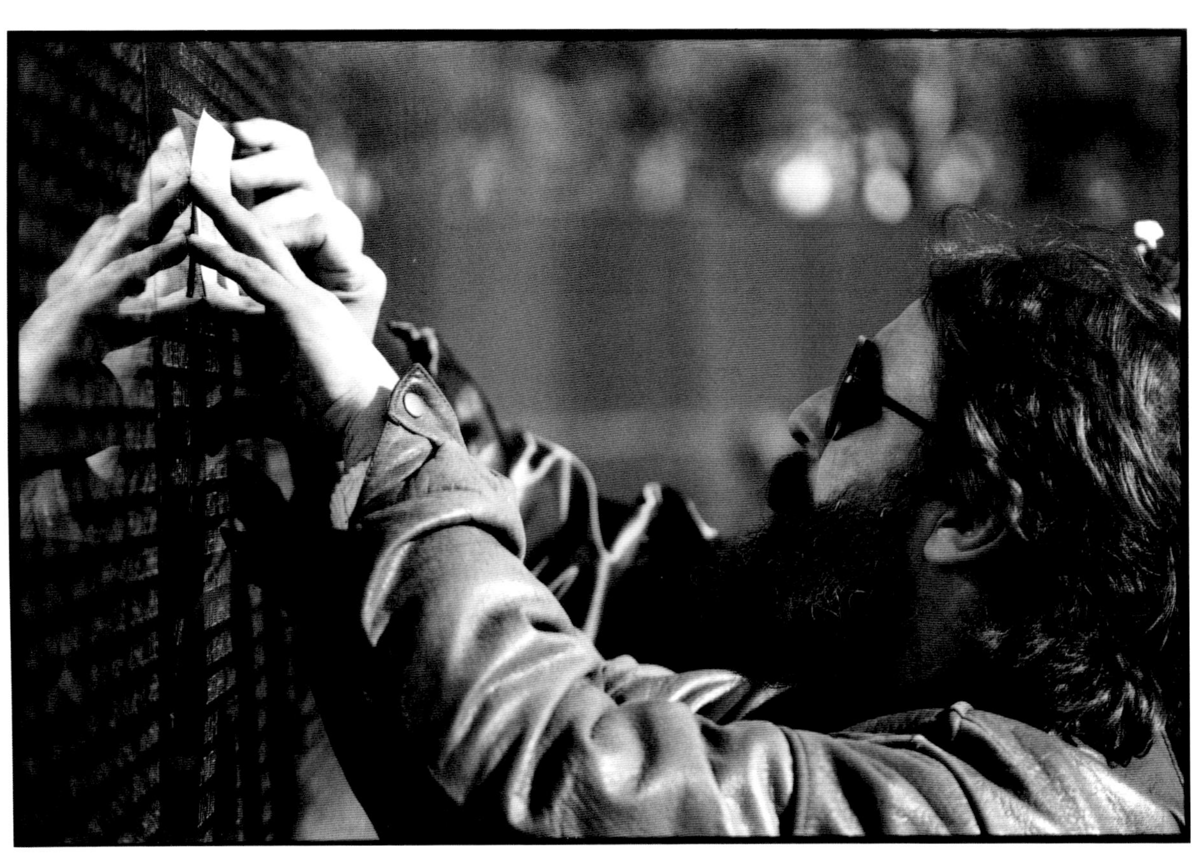

PLATE 18

1998

Remembrance 1987

How is it that I remember not one on this tragic Wall?

How is it possible that I remember not one name on this tragic wall? After all, there are ten tall panels that represent the year I spent in Nam.
My God, I hated to see you so hurt, so frightened and so sick.
How is it possible that I cannot remember any of you dying?
I grieve for you my nameless patients, and I grieve as well for your loved ones.
I also grieve for myself for I will never be free of tormenting uncertainty . . .
What should I have done and what could I have done to keep you from joining this heartbreaking roster of the dead?

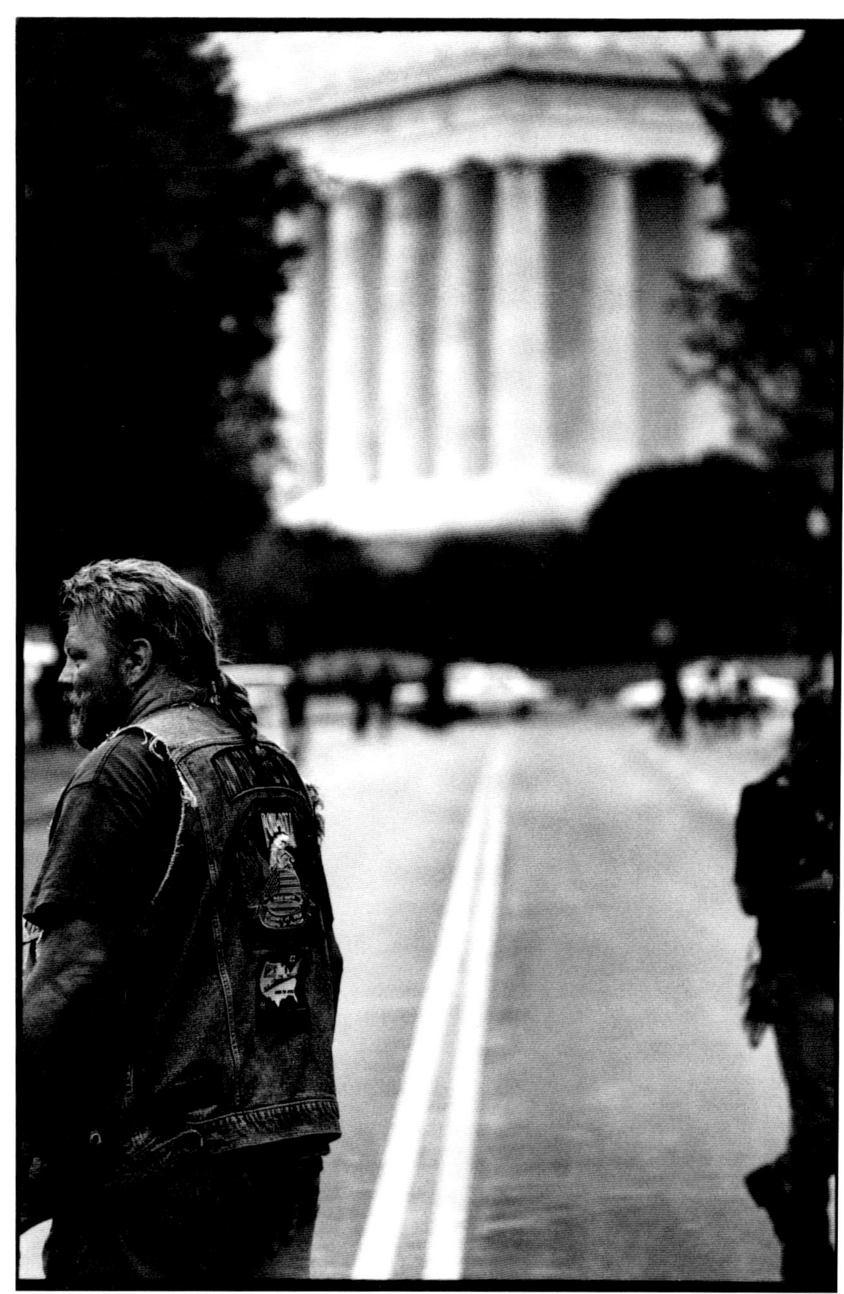

PLATE 19
1993

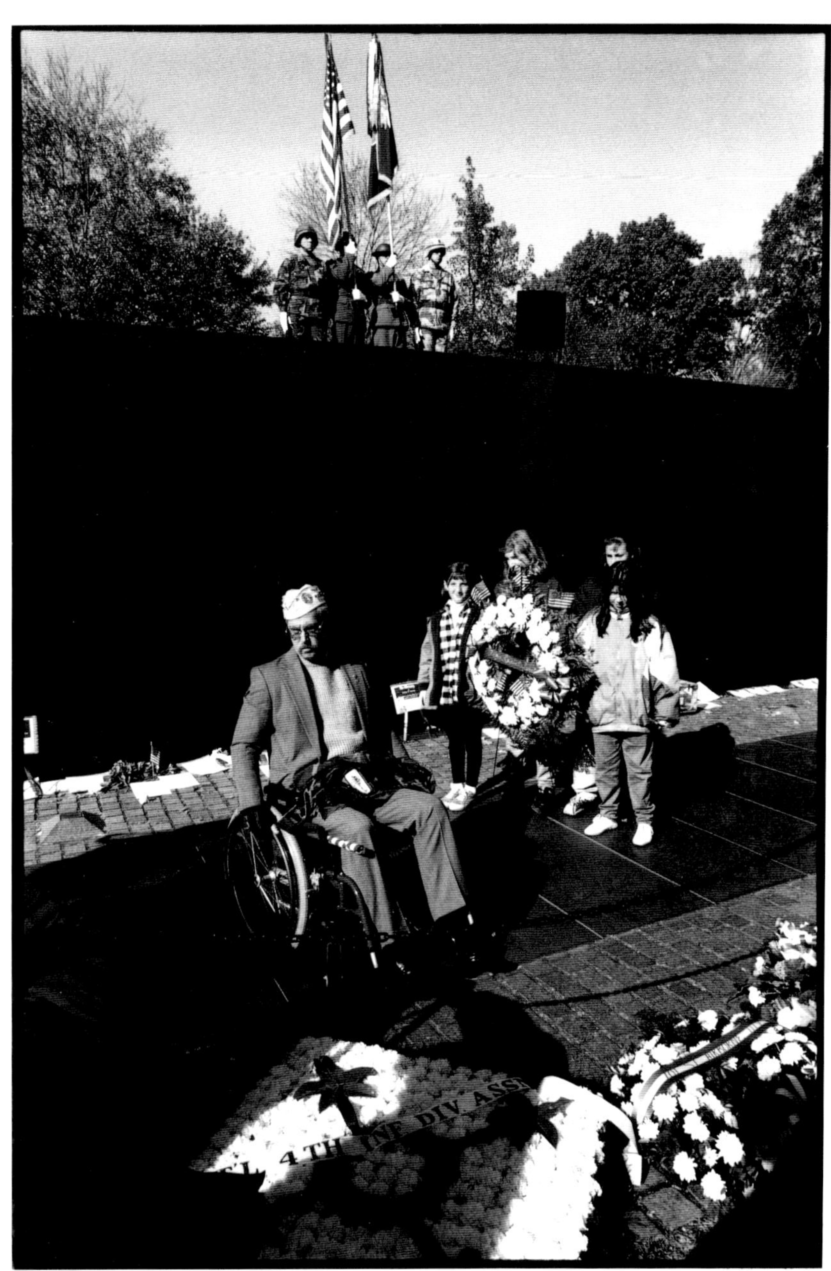

PLATE 20

1995

Thank you Lewis Puller
For trying so hard
For doing so much
Rest in peace our Brother

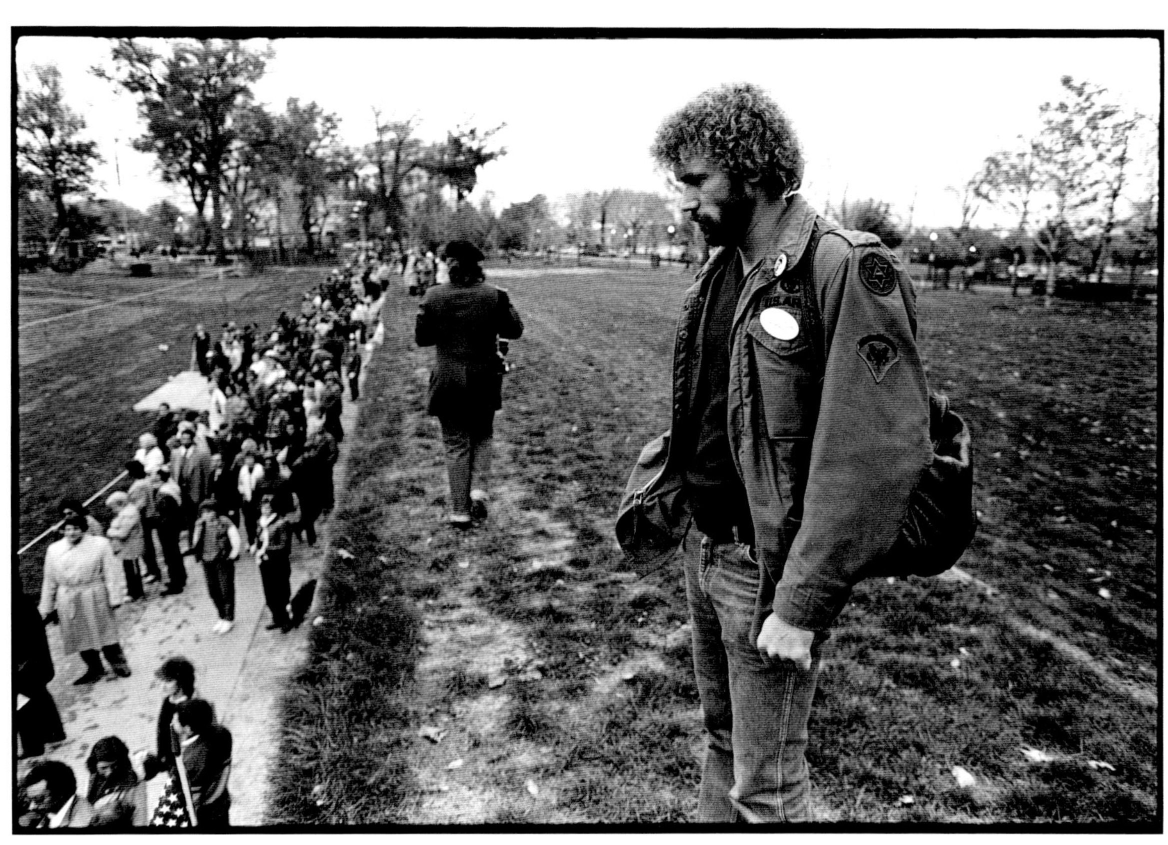

PLATE 21
1984

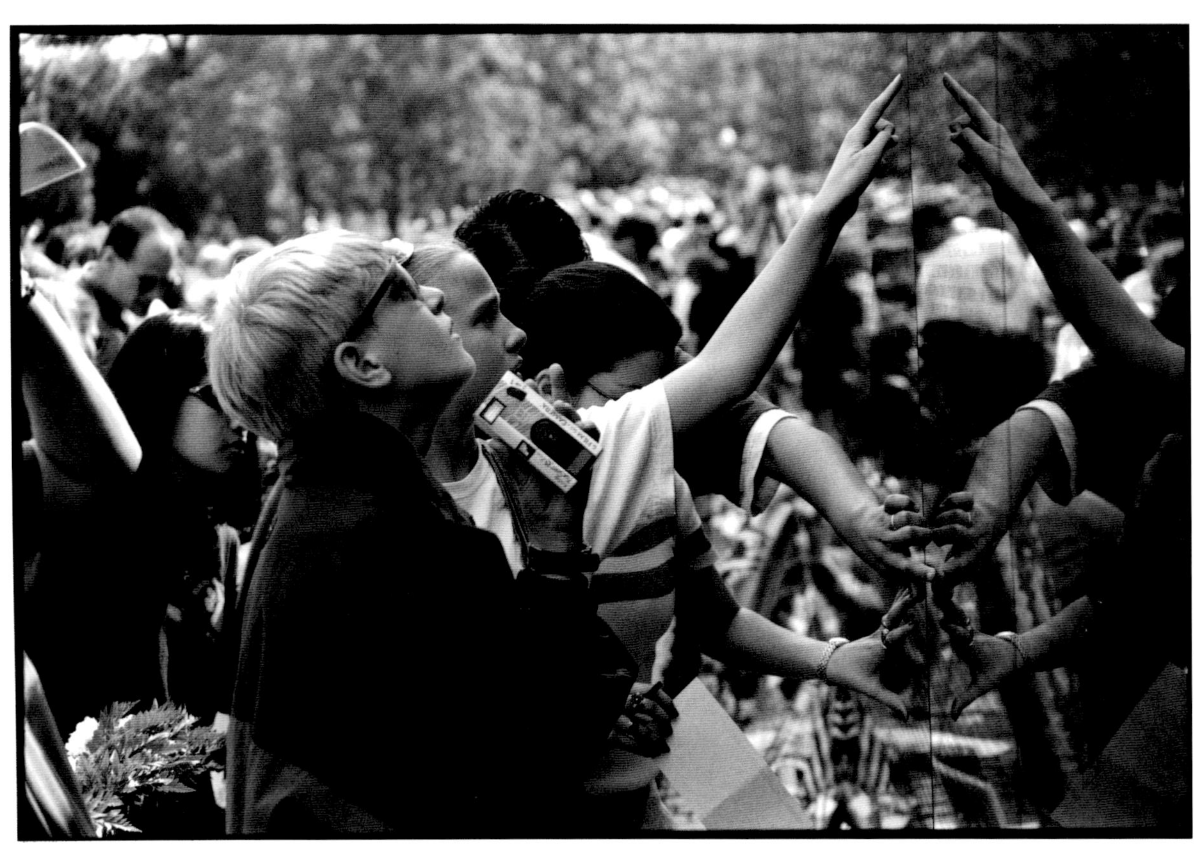

PLATE 22
1996

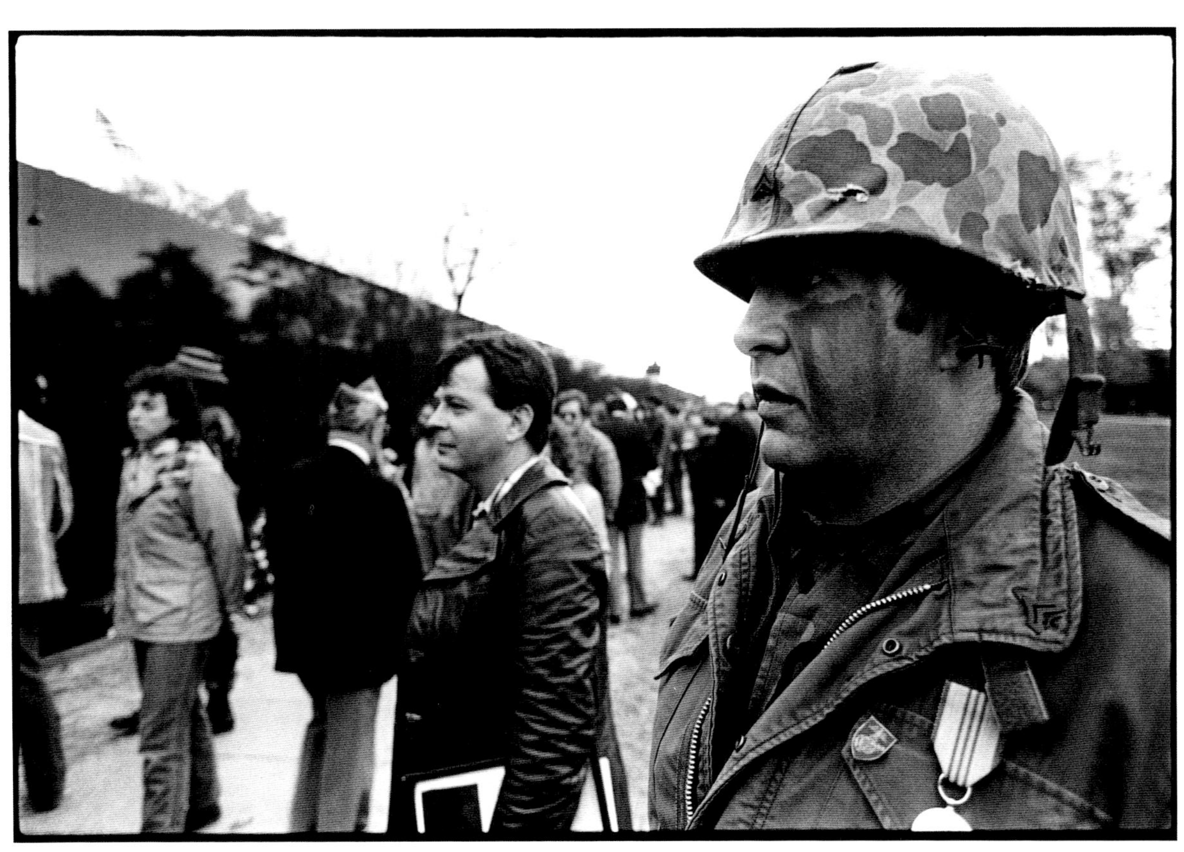

PLATE 23

1984

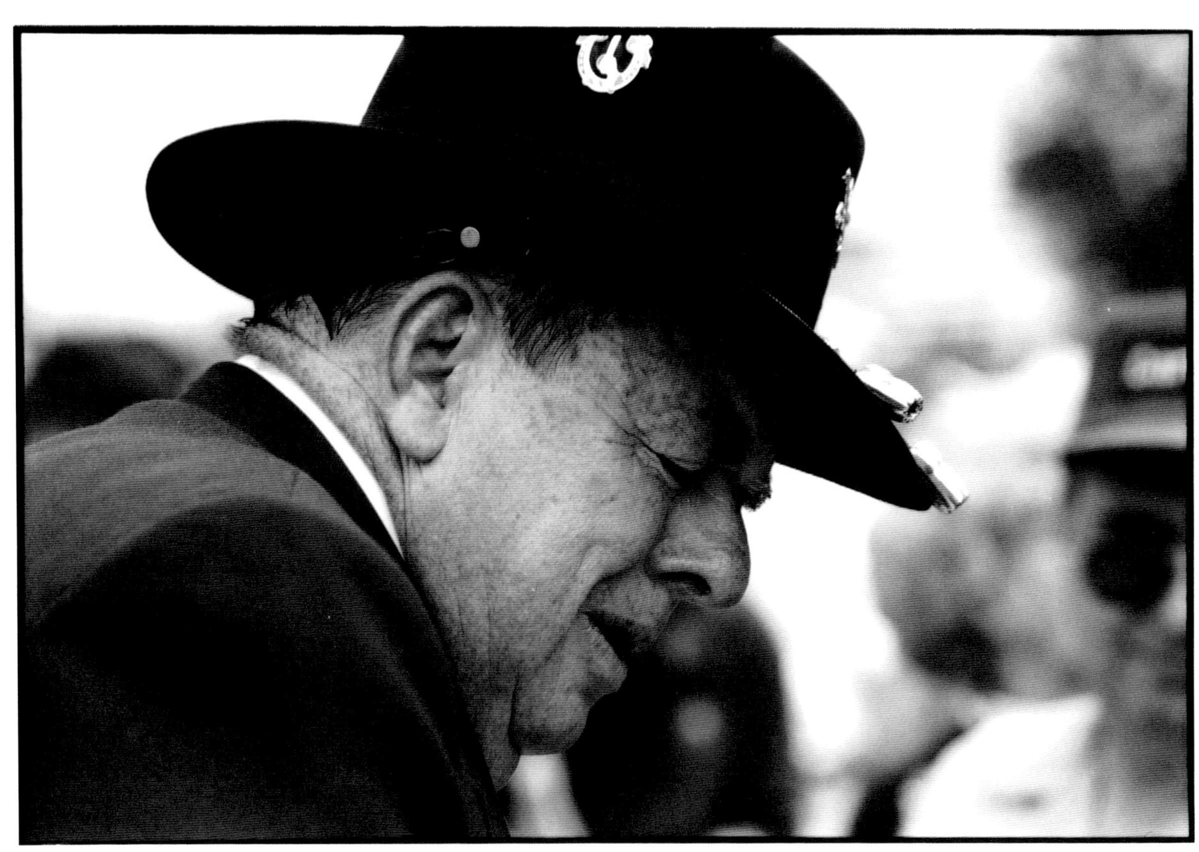

PLATE 24
1994

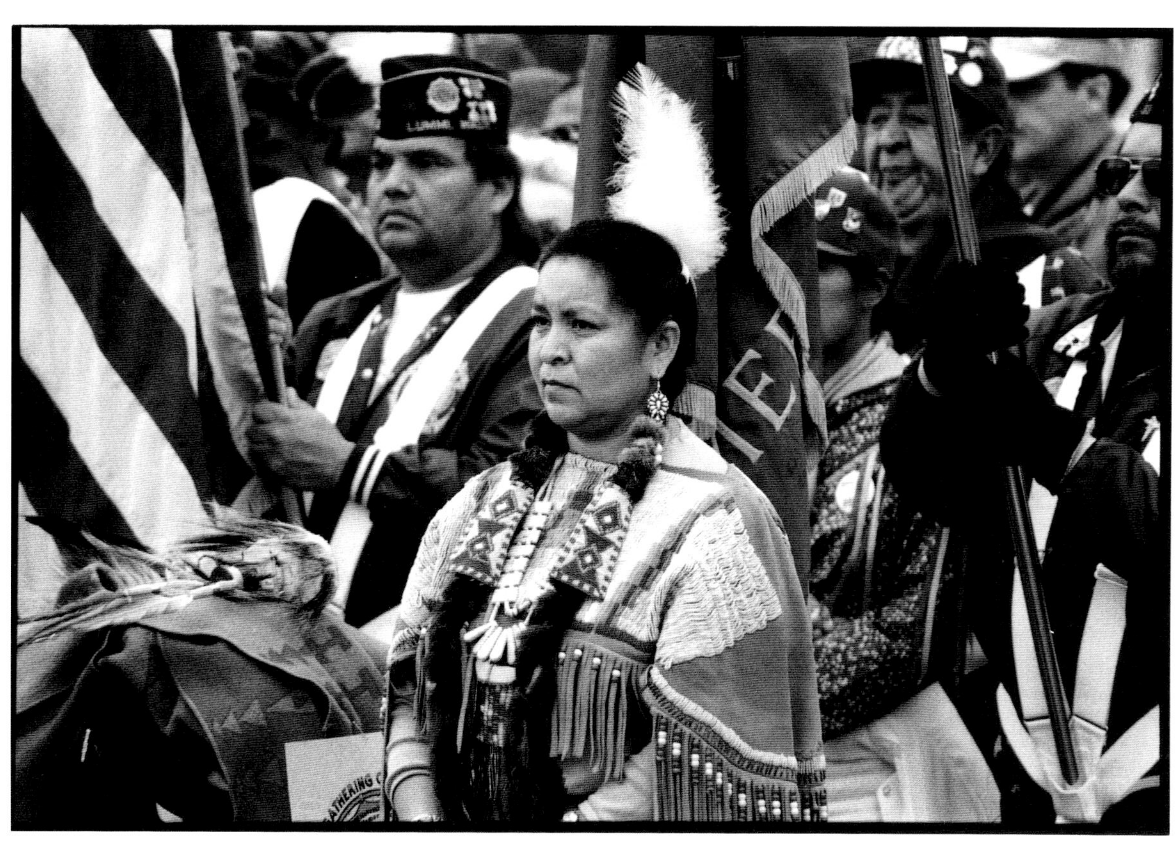

PLATE 25

1992

Dad, I came to visit you today, I haven't ever felt so close to you before. I never got a chance to know you, but I love you very much. There isn't a day go by mom doesn't think of you. Me and Gladene are always thinking of you too. You're gone from us now, but we'll all be together again one day. You'll never be forgotten, you still live in every one of us. I'm really proud to be your son, I hope I can be as good a man as you were. I love you dad.

I'll be back to see you if it's the last thing I ever do.

Your son, C.L., USN August, 1986.

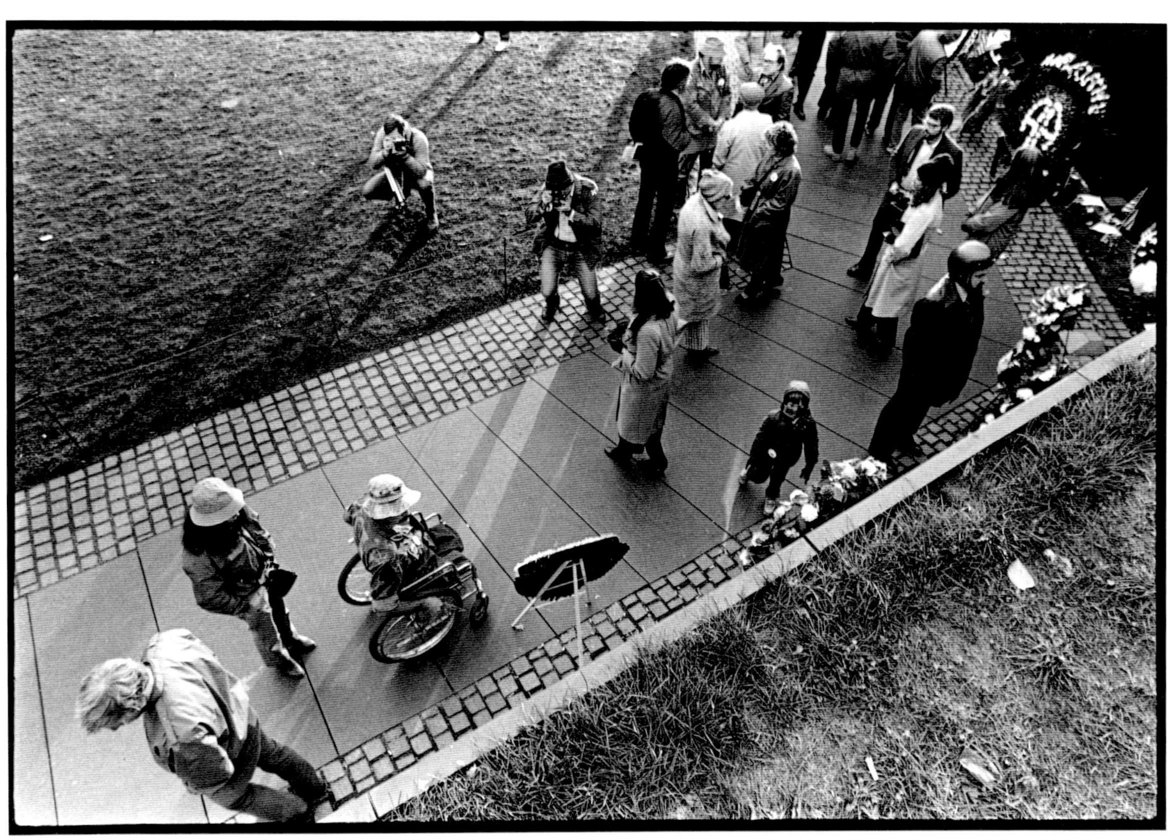

PLATE 26
1983

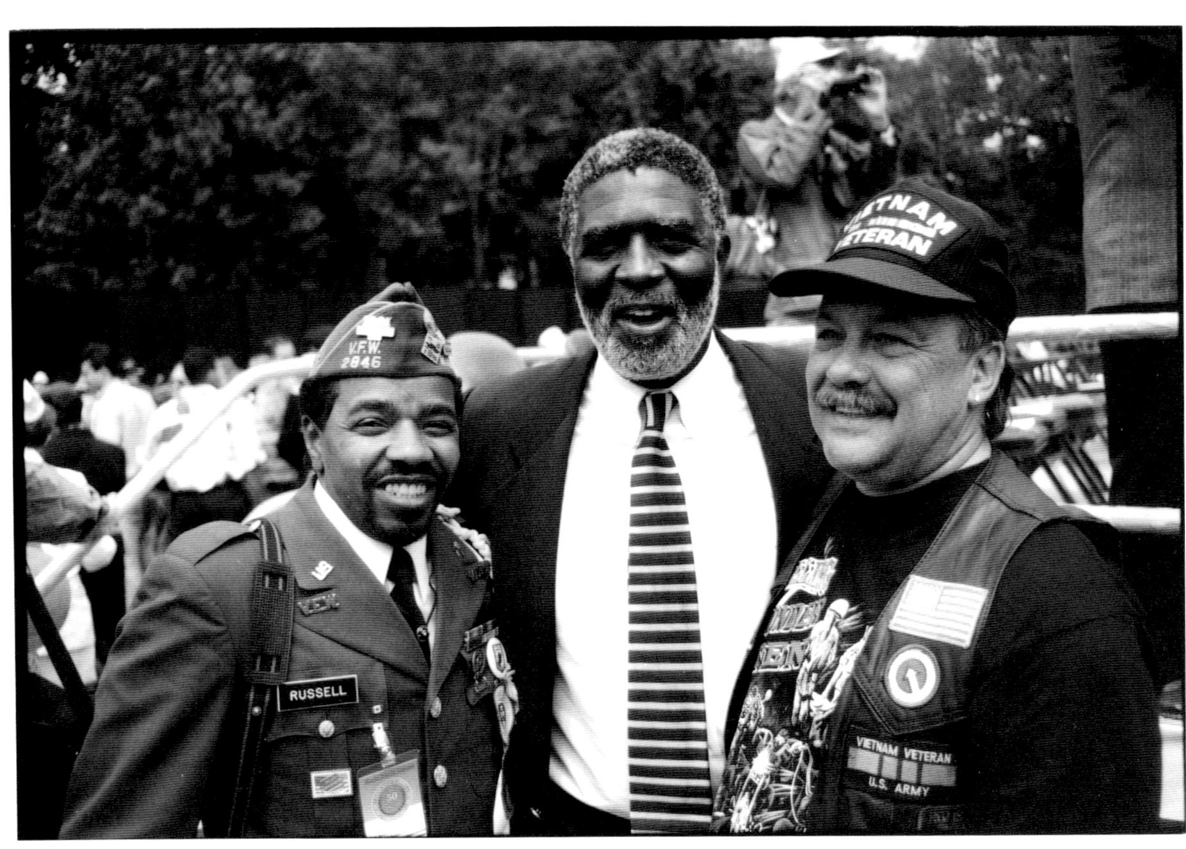

PLATE 27

1995

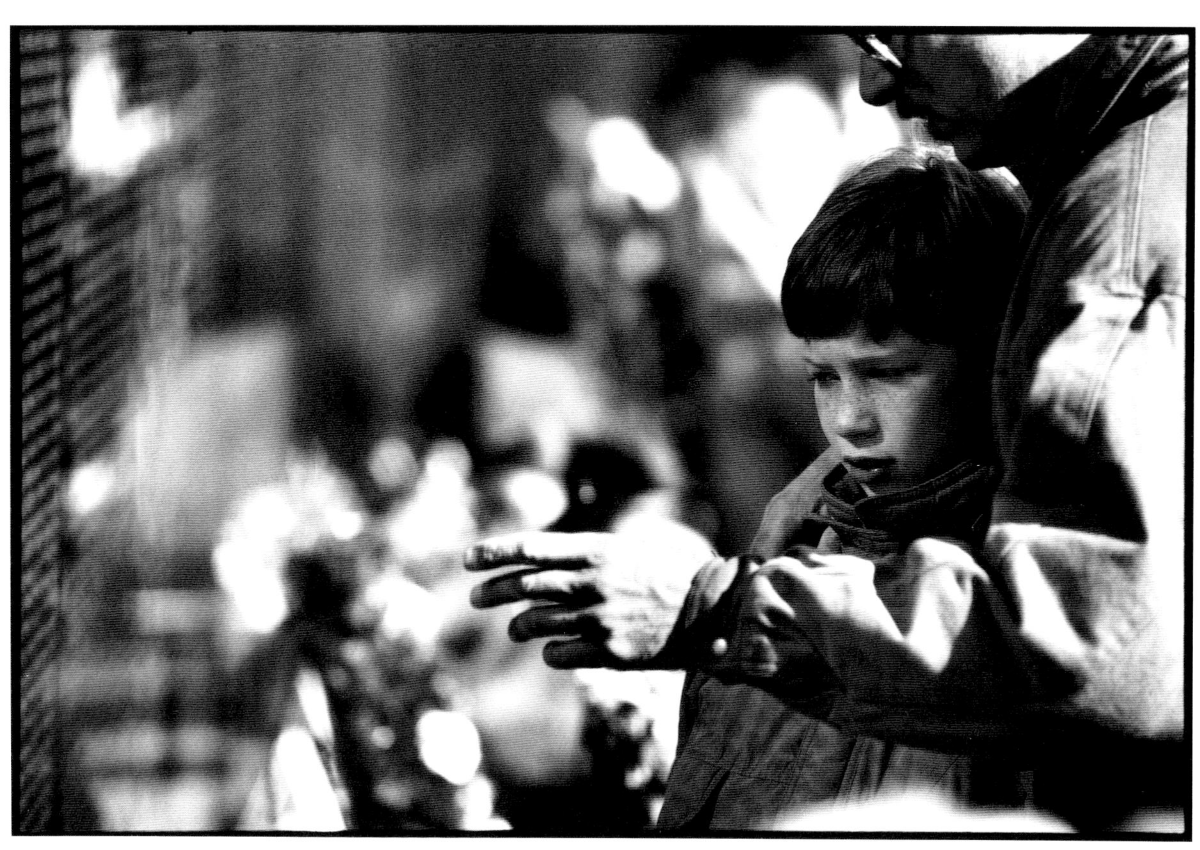

PLATE 28
1997

Sarge, It has been 22 years since I left you and all our comrades in the little country of Viet Nam.

It has taken me this long to be able to come and pay my respects to you and the rest of the troopers of the Herd who fought and died so courageously. I miss you all and I have not forgotten you. I am here today to say God Bless You. This warrior's hat I leave as a gift for you, and all our fallen troopers, with all the love and respect I have in my heart to call upon and give.

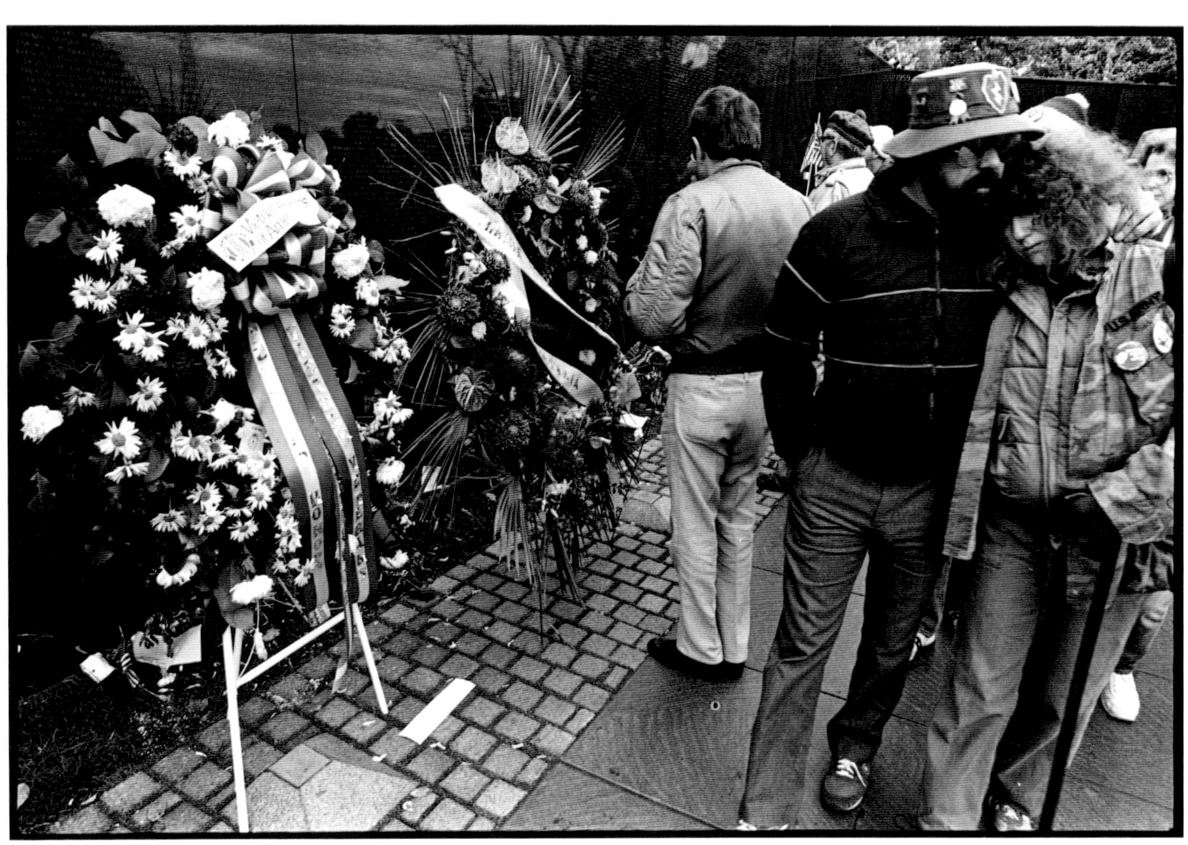

PLATE 29
1987

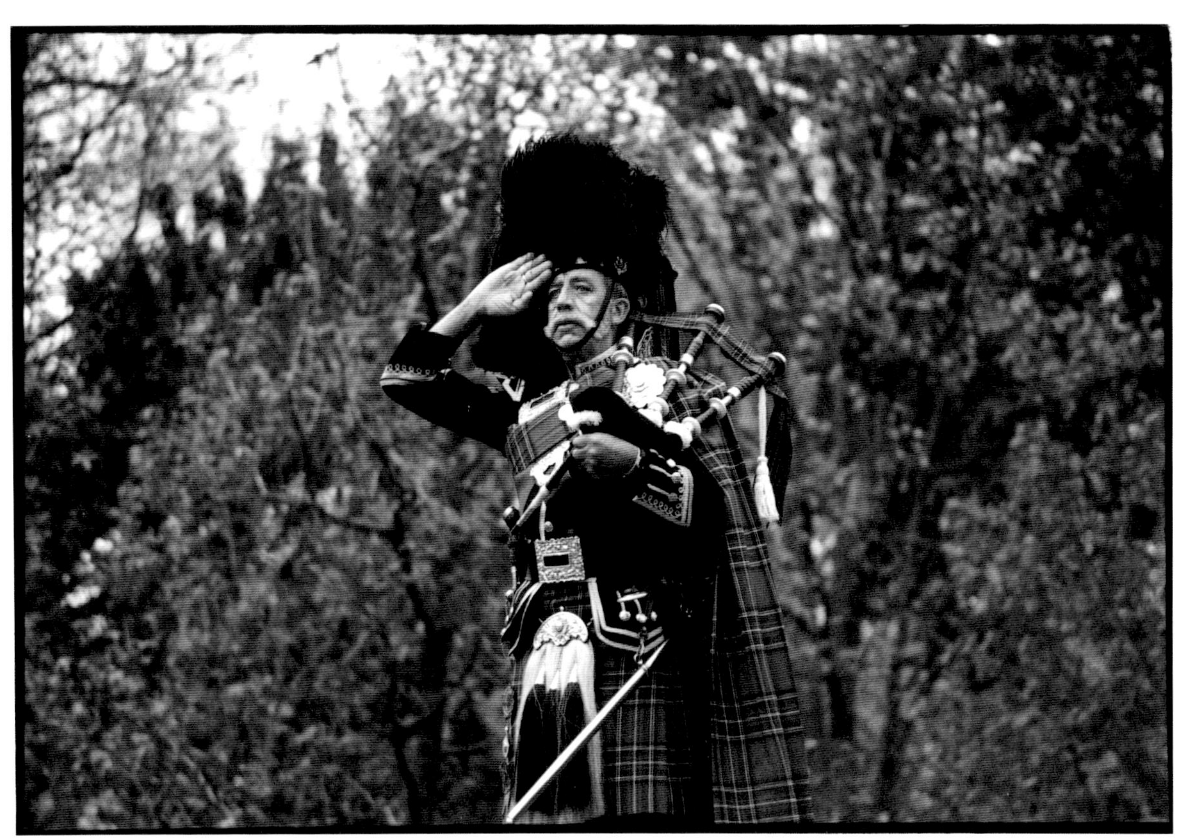

PLATE 30

1993

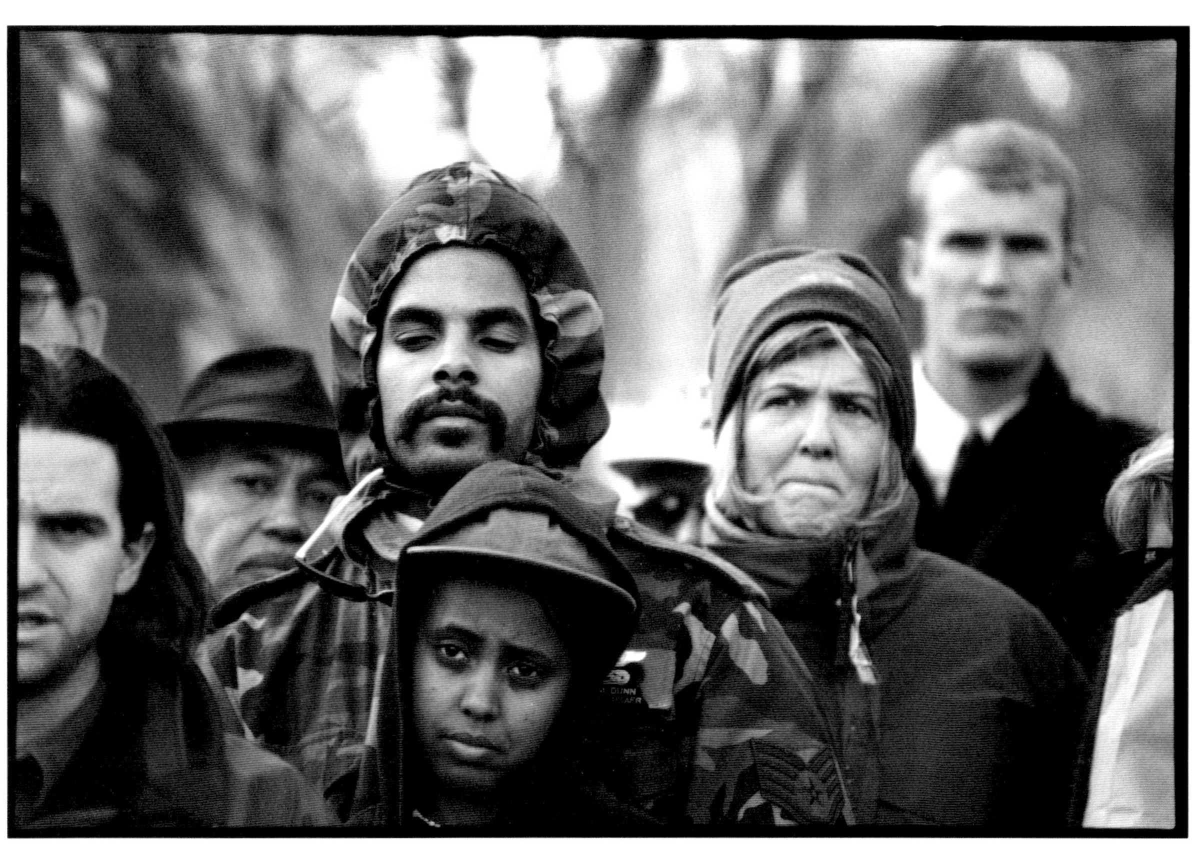

PLATE 31

1994

Pablo:

Me Amigo, You took my place on the ambush, I stayed behind, you died, I lived. Your spirit I'll carry with me always, and I'll share you with others. (4 June, 1967: KIA) I loved you.

Bob USMC

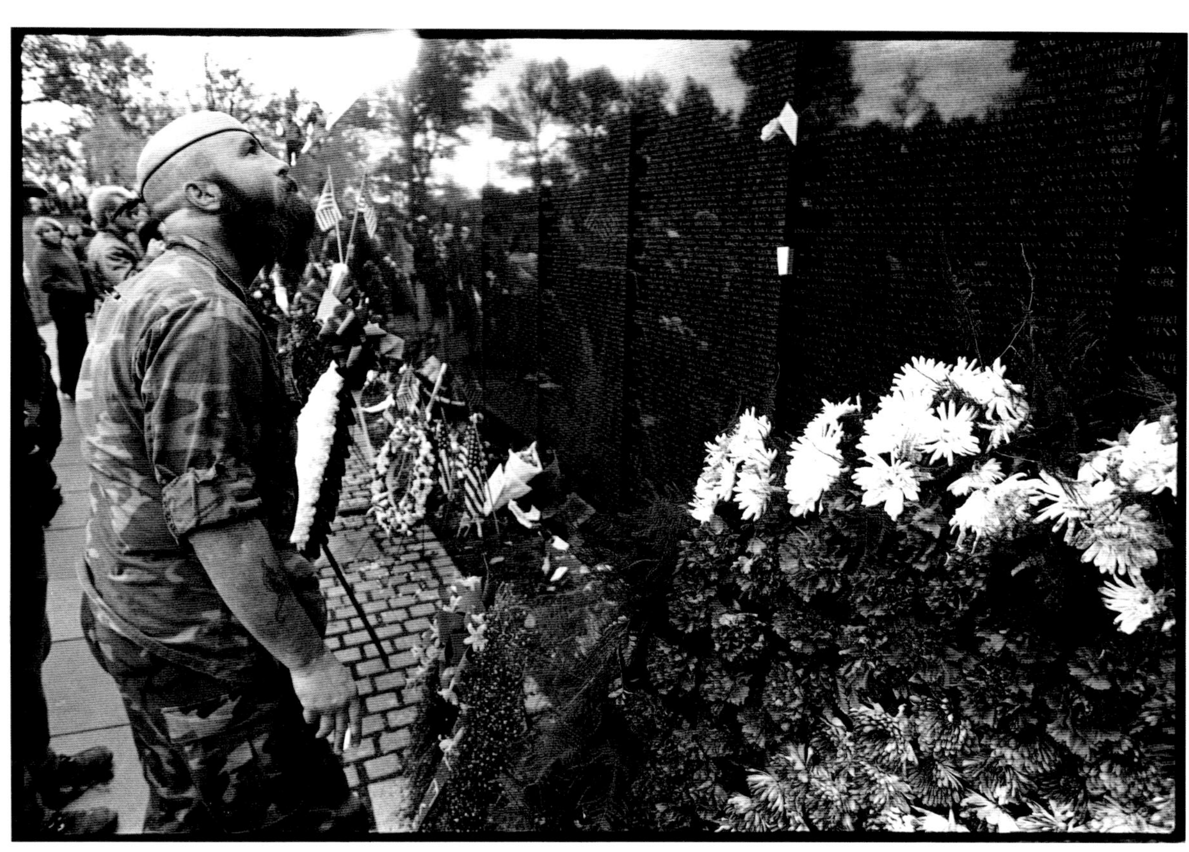

PLATE 32

1984

Jimmy:

To my dear uncle. I'll never know you but I will always love you. You are sadly missed. I just wish I would have met you.

Love, your niece

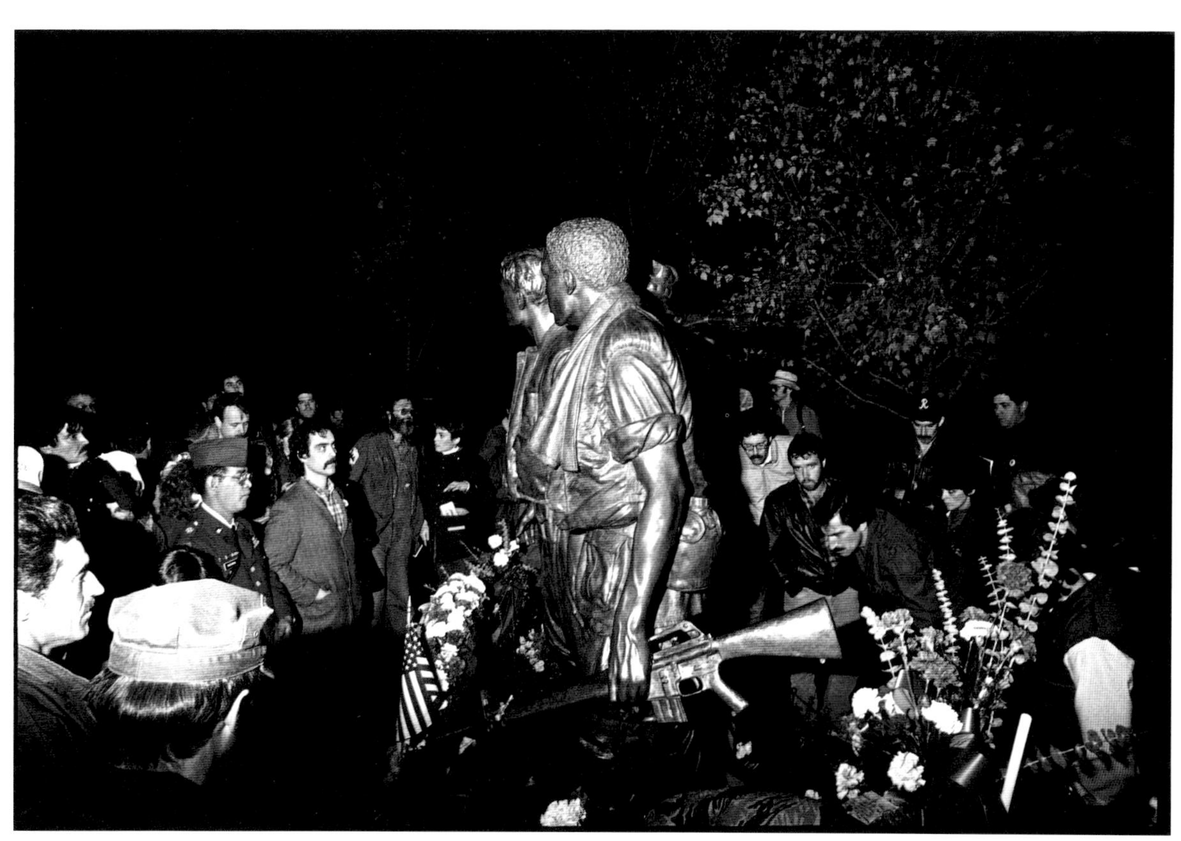

PLATE 33
1984

Donald,

My son was 4.9 years old the day the Marines drove you past the house on the way to your final rest. He and Betsy and Theresa and Frankie lined up on the curb. Mark saluted you as you passed. That memory will live within always. How proud you would have been of him, for you loved the Marines so much. How proud we were of you then and now.

A Friend In Life

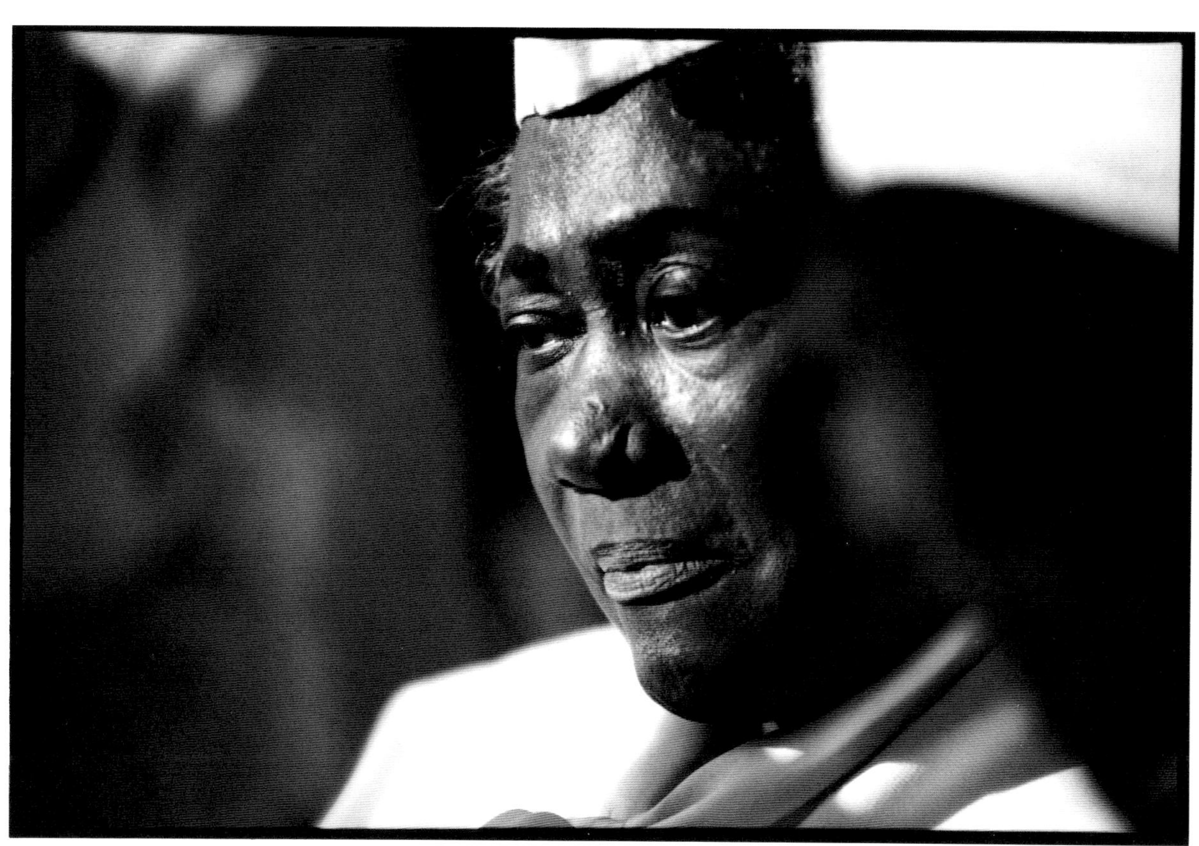

PLATE 34
1988

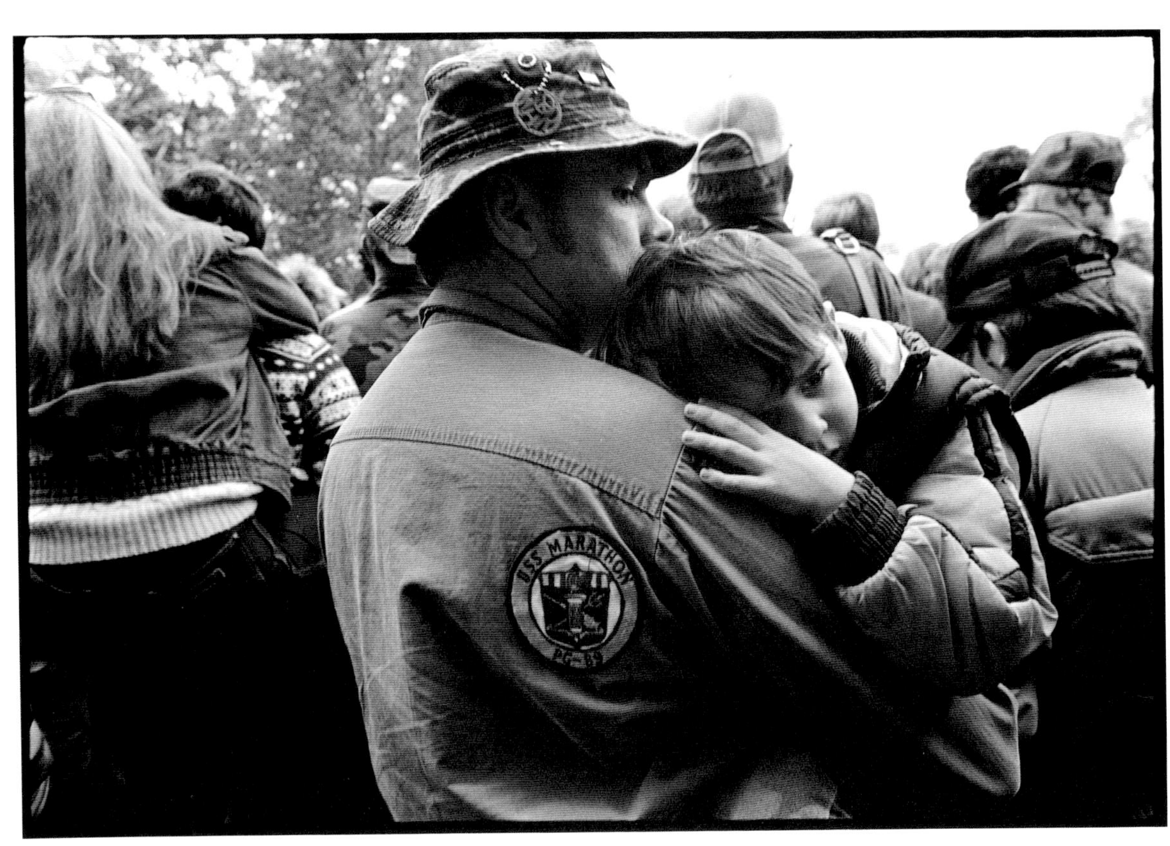

PLATE 35
1989

Dear Benny:

Twenty-five years ago you carried my PRC 10 while you and I were the only "round eyes" with a 150 Ruff-Puffs. We shared many long walks, some night ambushes, more than one deep water crossing and too many "monkey bridges." You were a good RTO but a very shitty swimmer as we found out the hard way. You were also mostly blind w/o your glasses as we found out the same day you about drowned while trying to do a deep crossing!

I really tried to write your family but never got much on paper that made sense. I have always told my self that my words could probably never bring much comfort to those that loved you! I used to really wonder how come you took three hits and I took none even though we were less than three feet apart?

Robert

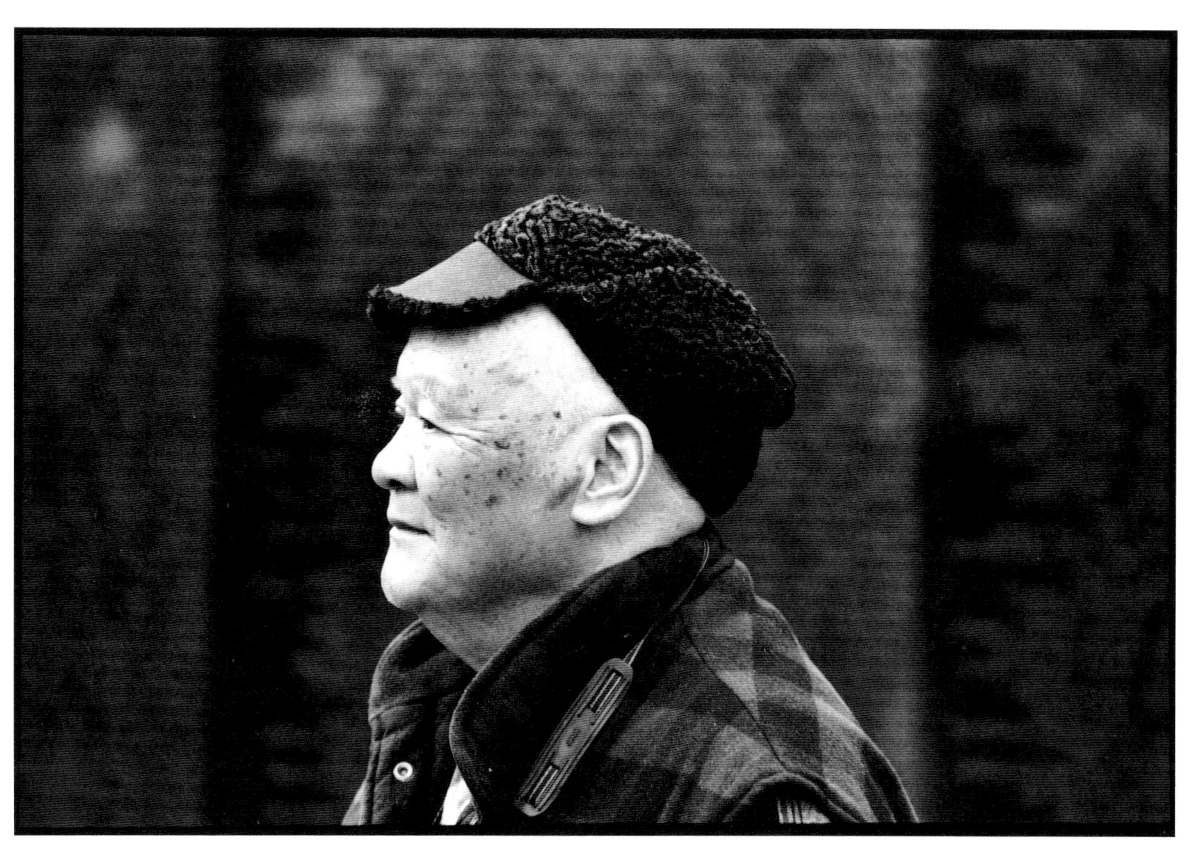

PLATE 36
1989

In 1960 Bobby, we met on our first day of high school. As freshmen we fought for the same position on the football team, we took opposing sides in our presidential debates; you Kennedy, me Nixon.

For the next four years we studied, worked and played sports together. Coach Bowman finally realized that he needed us both in the line-up, so we assumed different positions.

After graduation, you went away to college and I went in the army. Little did I know that war would bring us together again some years in the future, at least this time we were in agreement, our nation called and we answered. I was home from my second tour when you left for yours.

Bobby, I came home and you didn't. So many times I think of you and your smile and your love of life and your love for Judy.

Bobby, our Bible tells us "That greater love hath no man, than he who lays down his life for his friends." I hope that everyone who passes this wall realizes that.

Merry Christmas, Bobby and Peace!

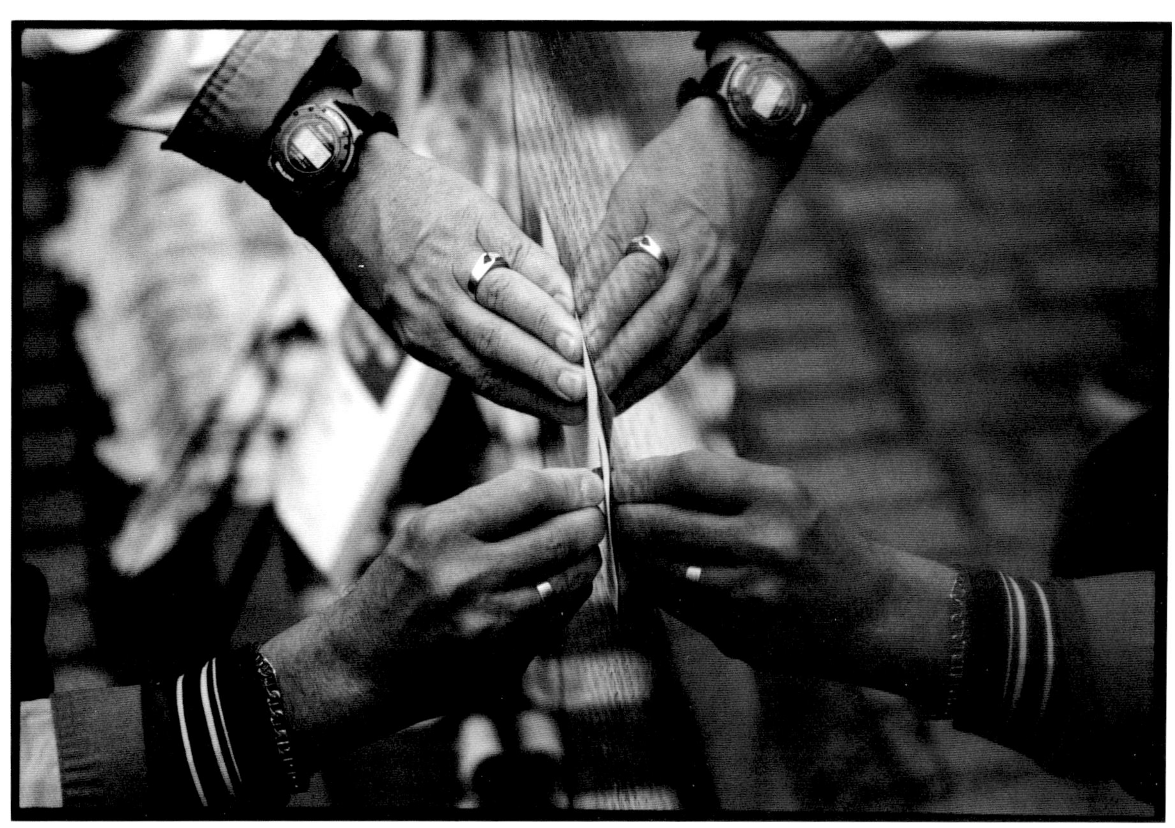

PLATE 37
1997

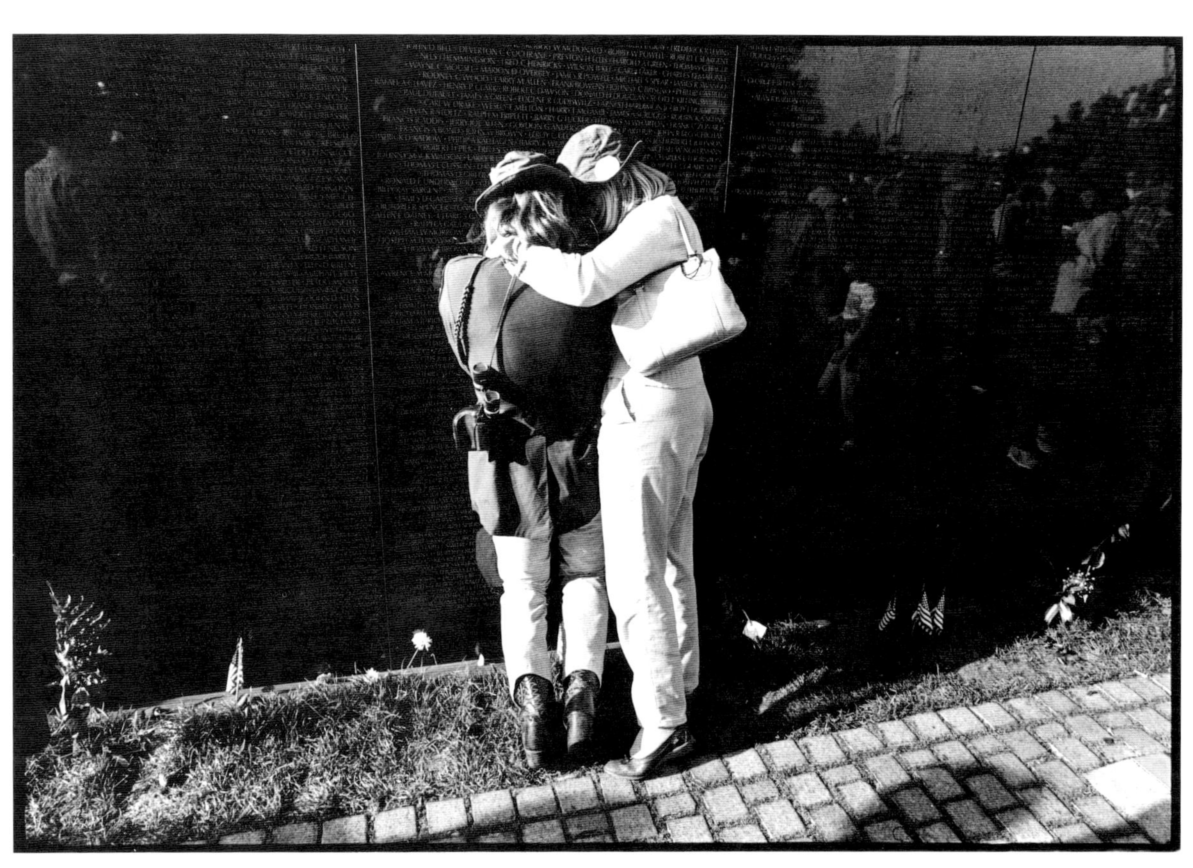

PLATE 38

1983

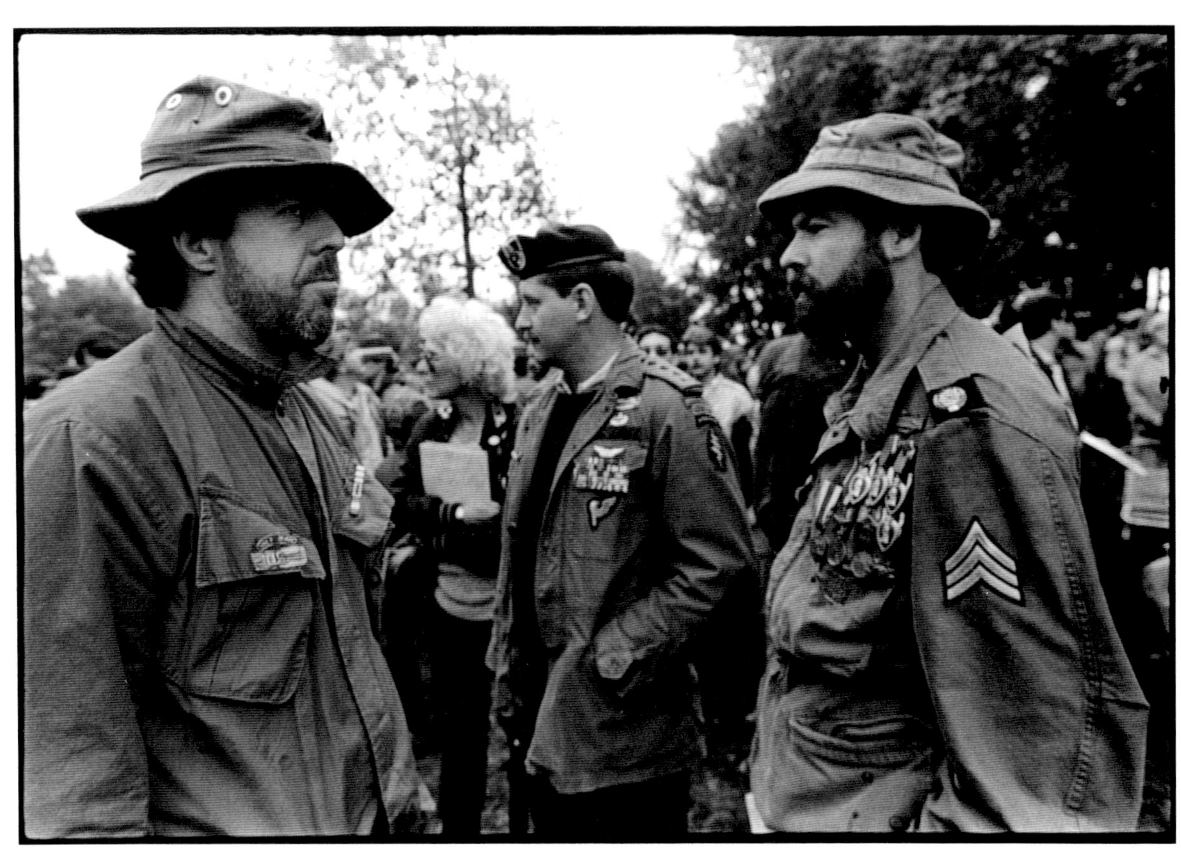

PLATE 39

1983

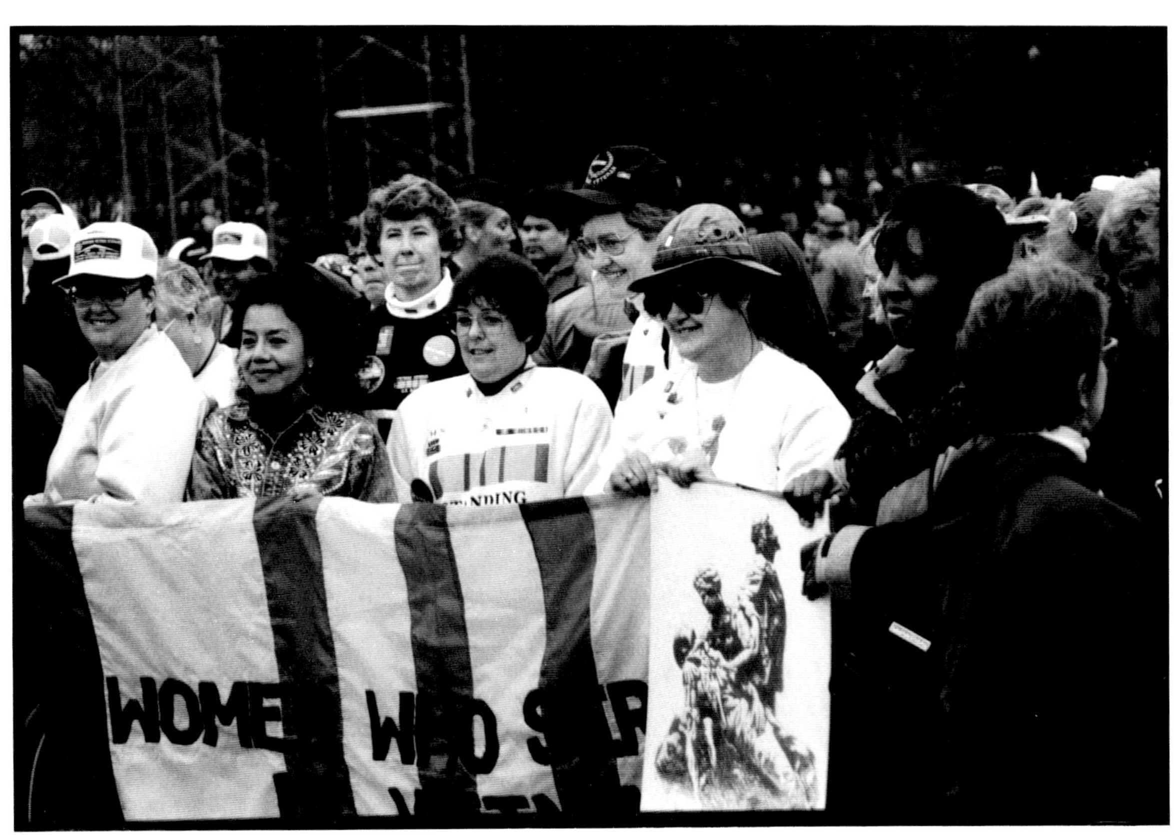

PLATE 40
1992

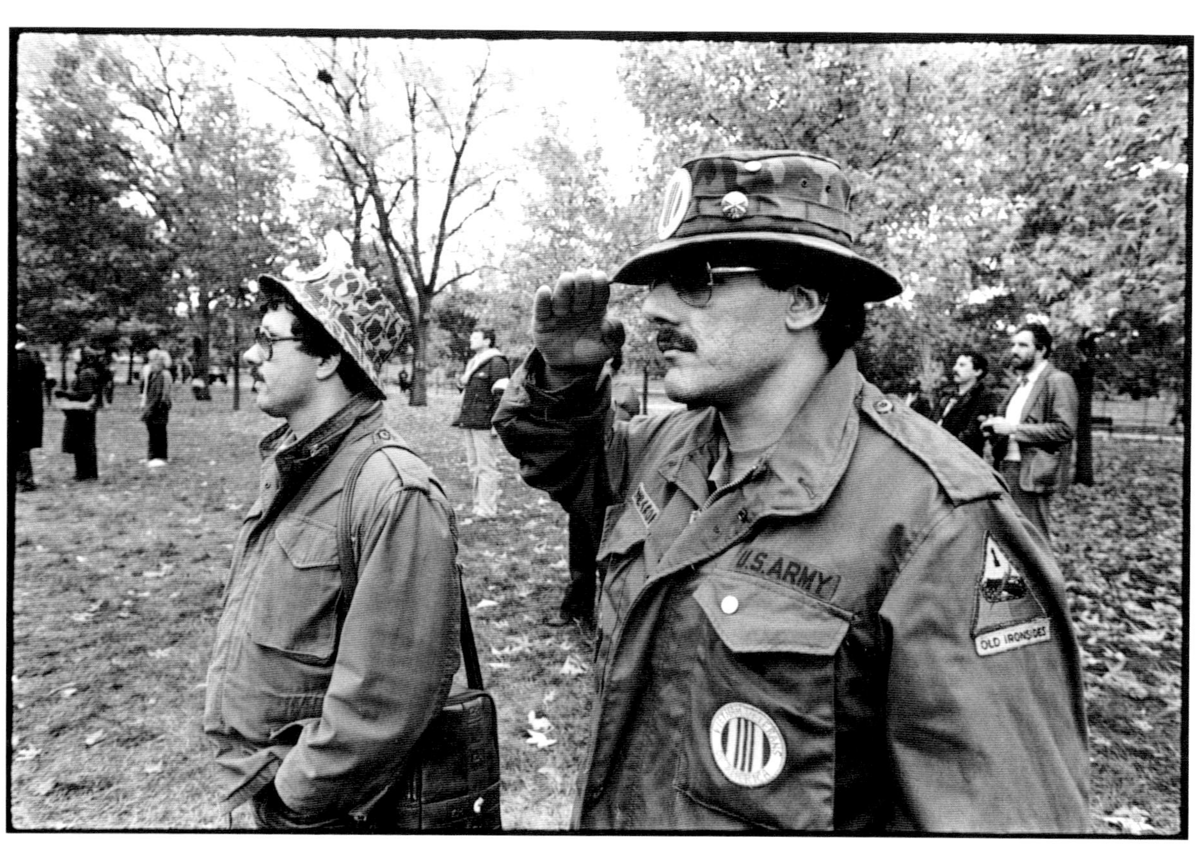

PLATE 41

1986

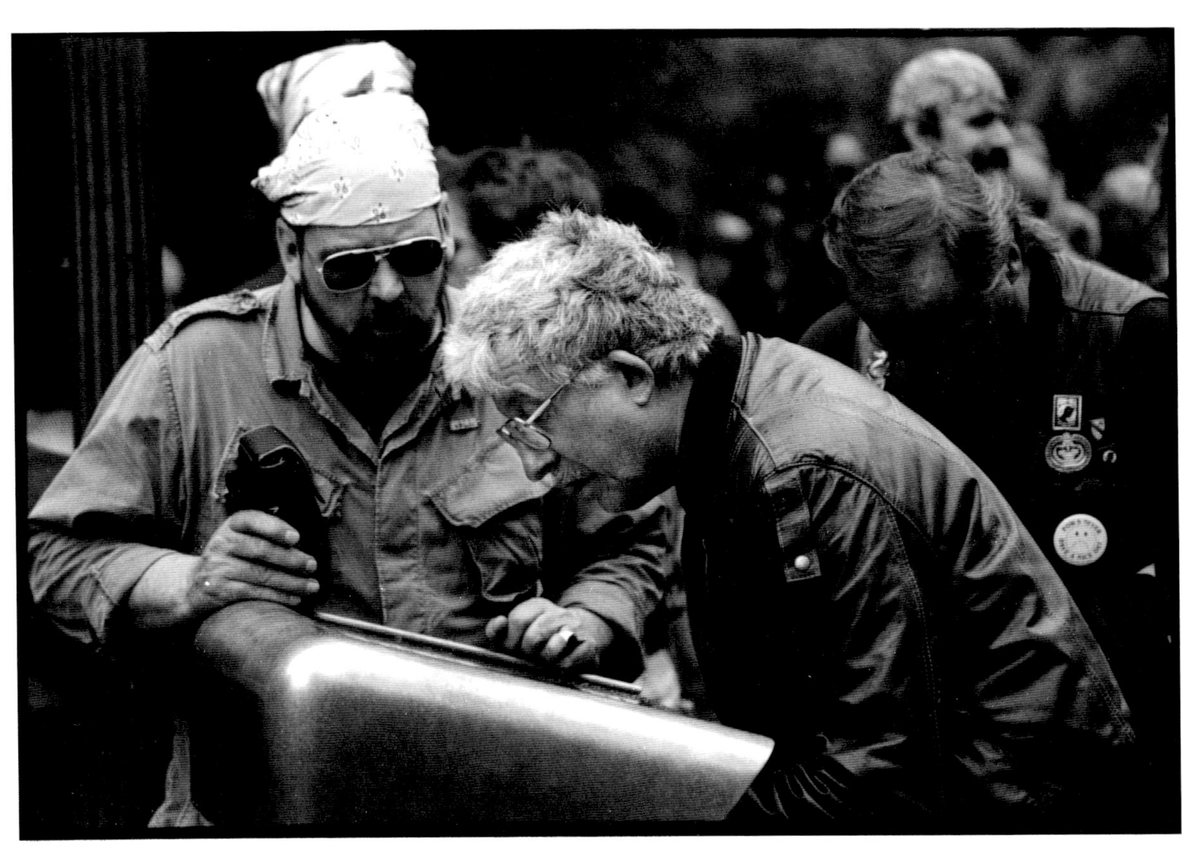

PLATE 42

1991

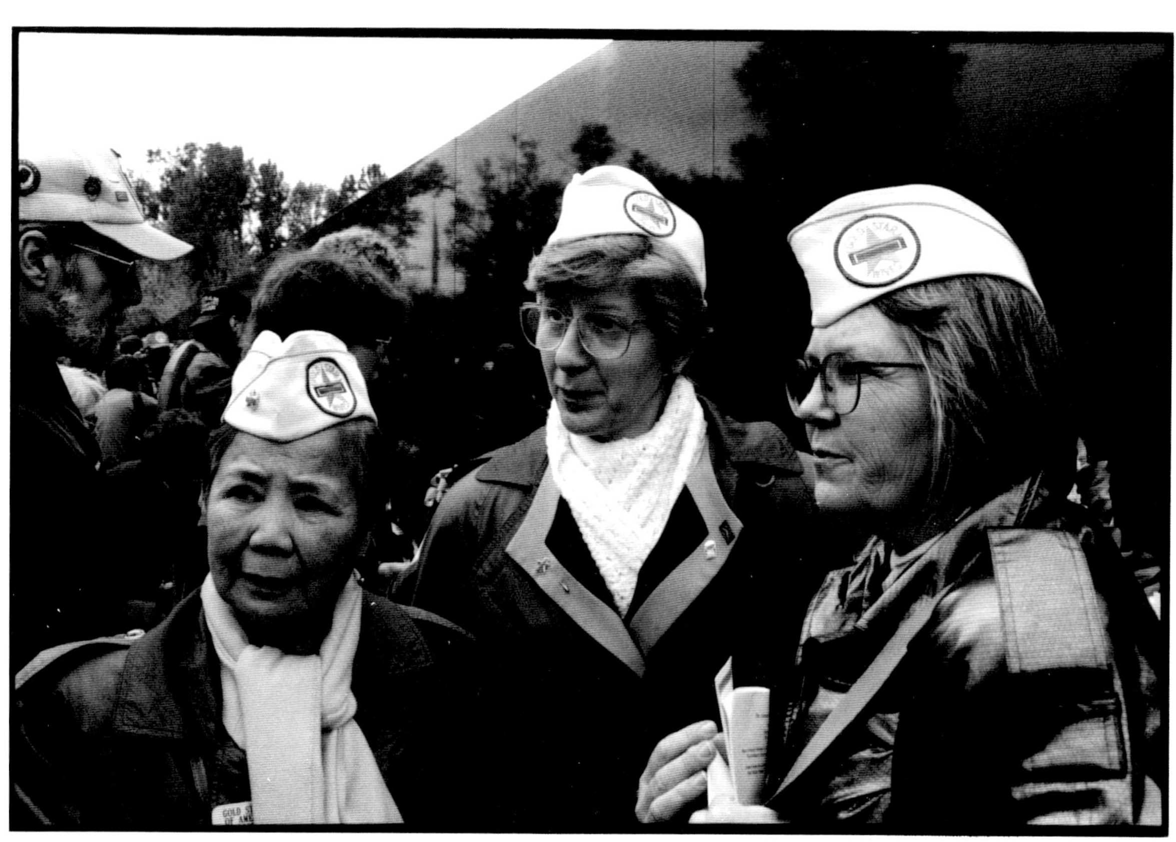

PLATE 43

1996

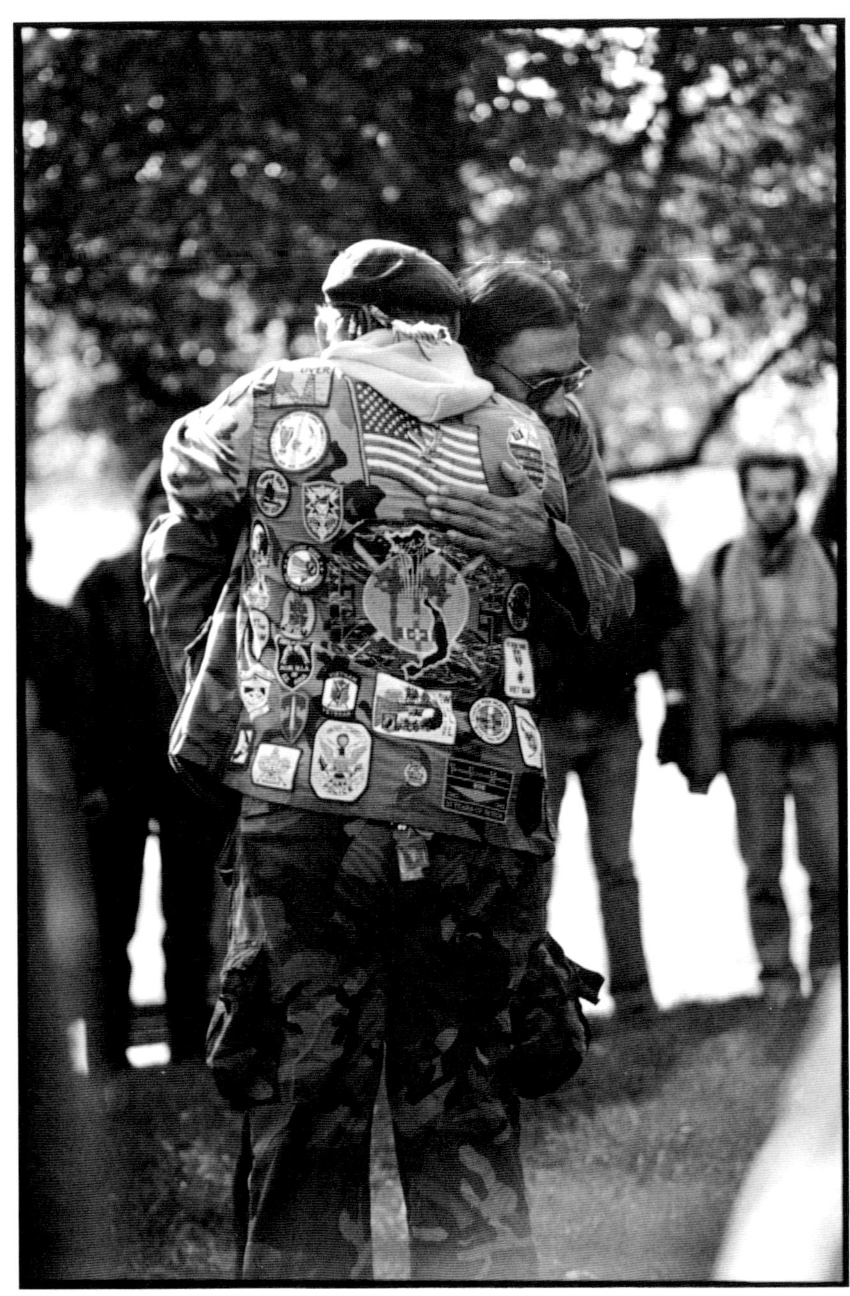

PLATE 44

1995

Dear Ed:

It's taken me 22 years to get the courage, but I finally made it. There hasn't been one day in those 22 years that I haven't thought about you—talked to you, loved and missed you!

Till we meet again, and we will,

Kim

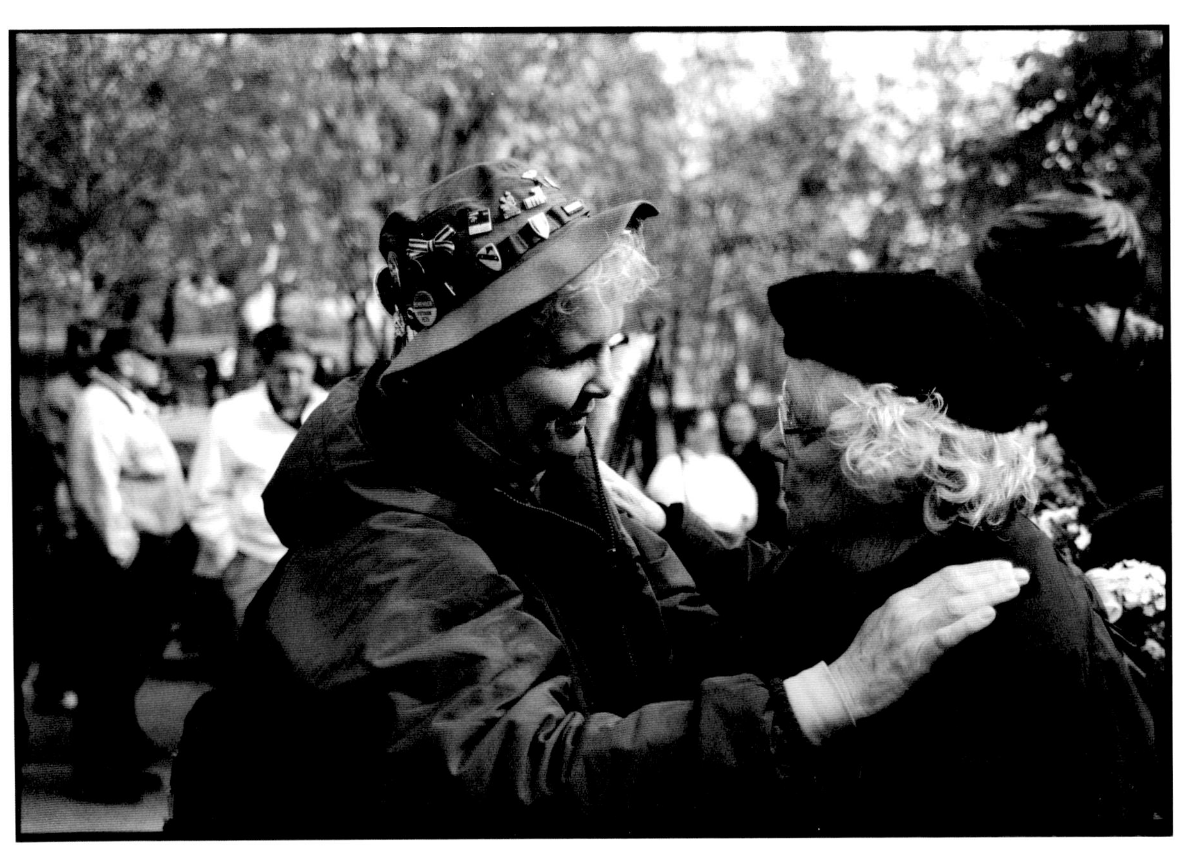

PLATE 45
1991

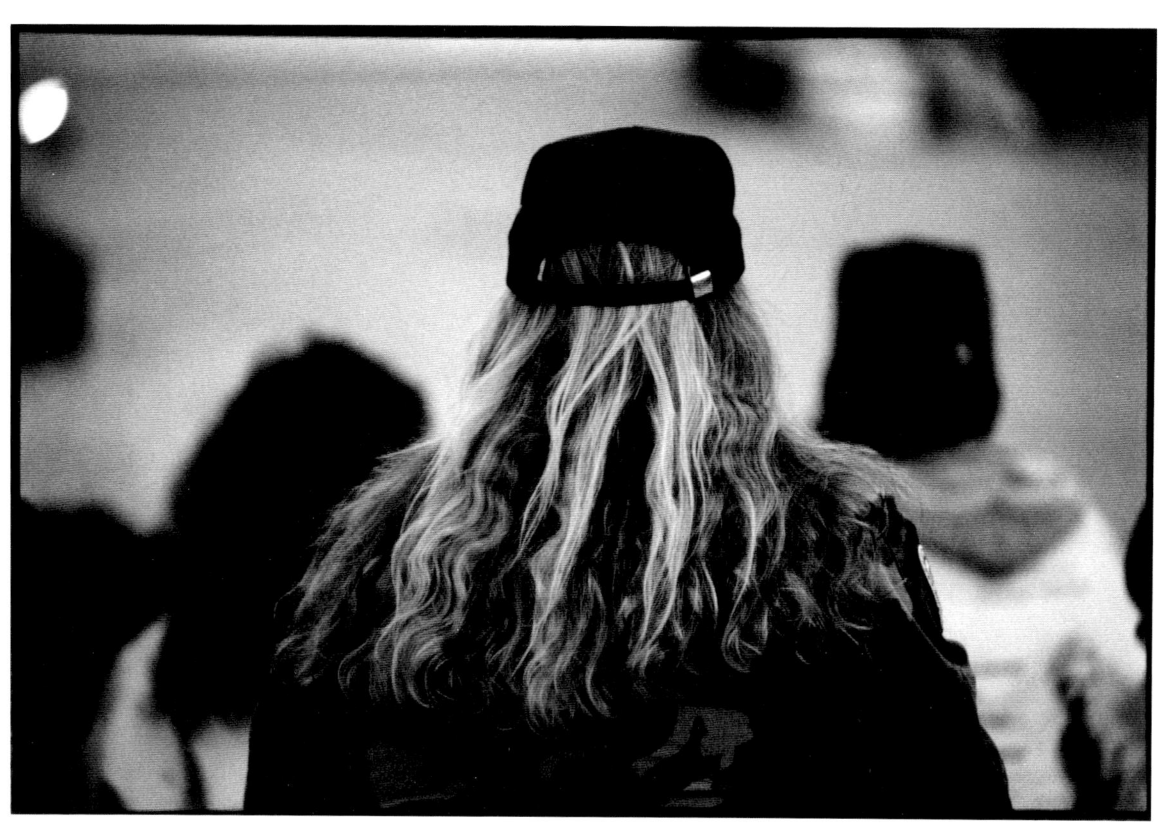

PLATE 46

1987

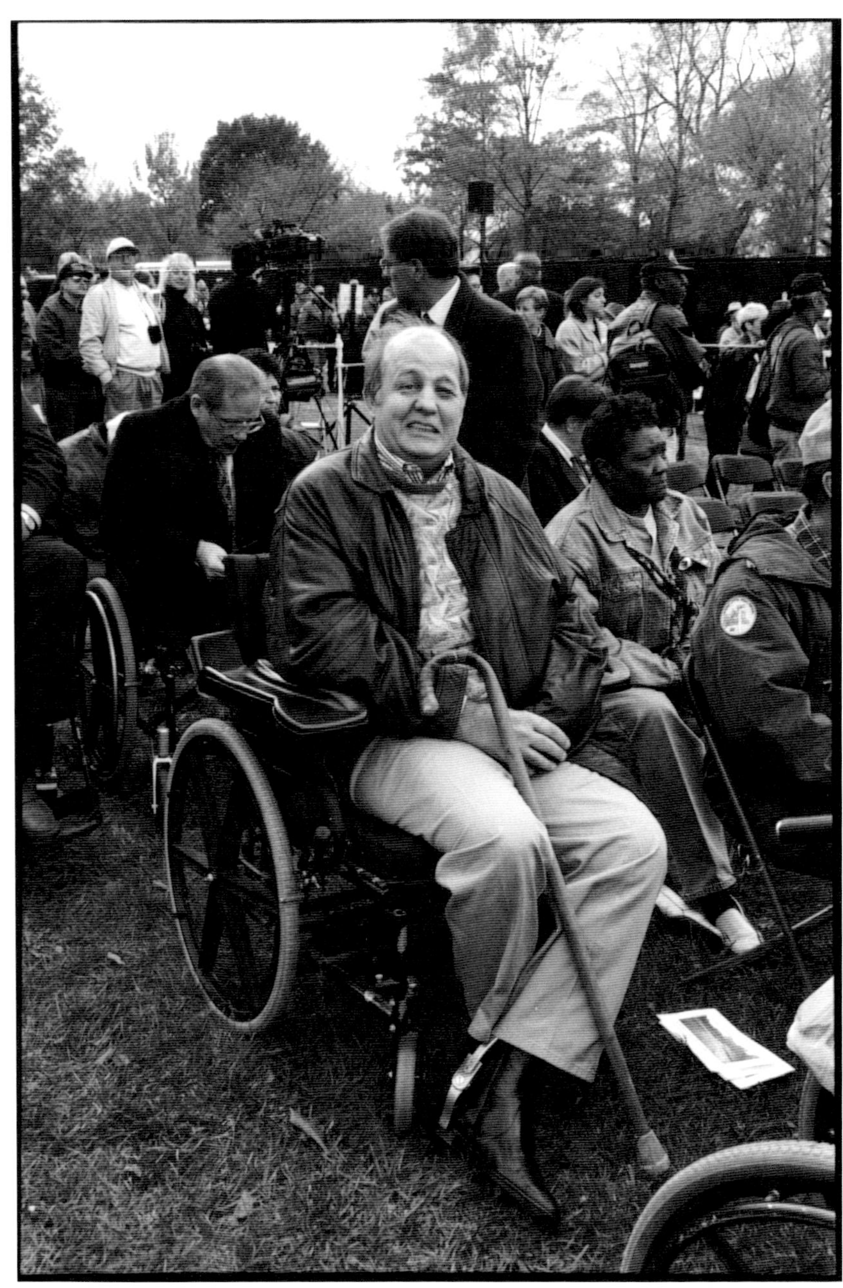

PLATE 47

1997

Its flawless marble gleams in the early morning sunlight. With the reflections of the sunlight on its black marble surface it almost looks wet, as are the eyes of those who look upon the wall with tears in their eyes. The mothers, fathers, brothers, sisters, friends and other relatives of the men who, at one time, belonged to these names that adorn this beautiful wall. I see my reflection here on the wall and wonder why . . . why did all these men have to die?

WHY?!

Katrina

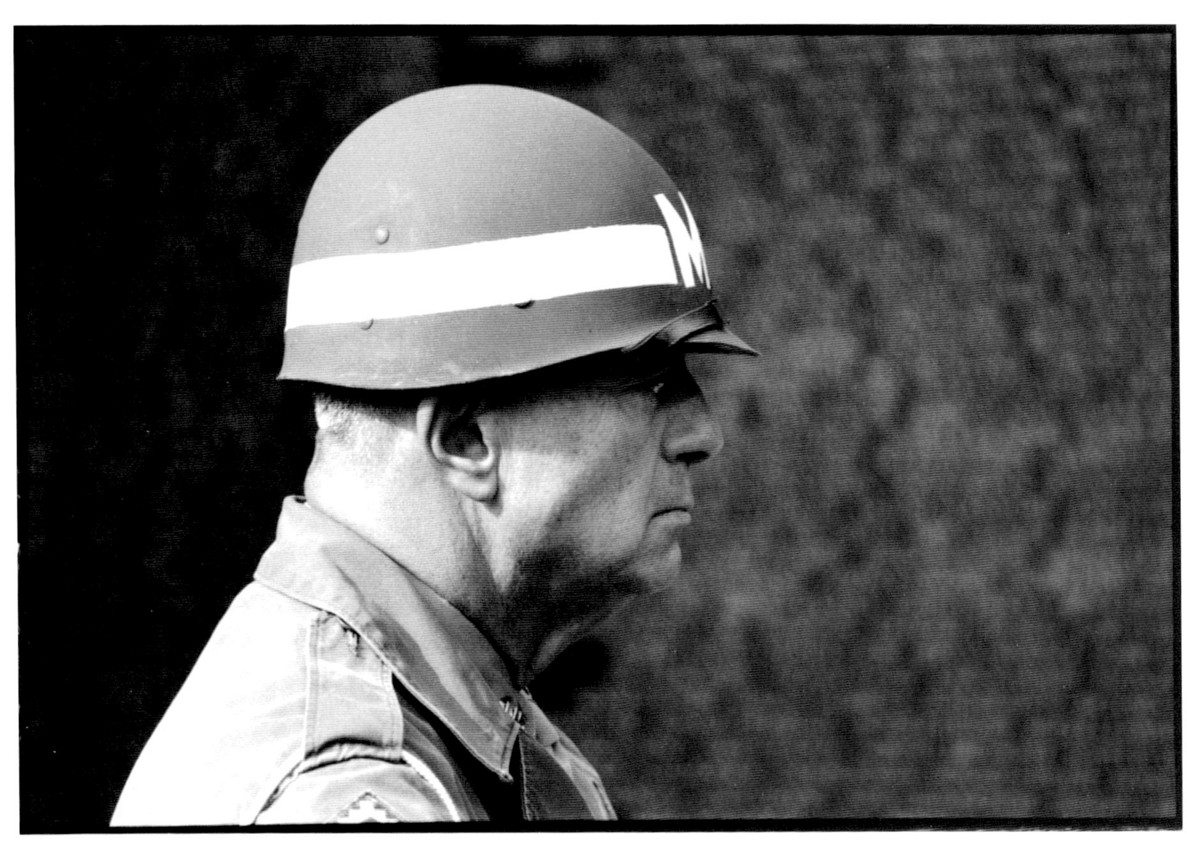

PLATE 48
1996

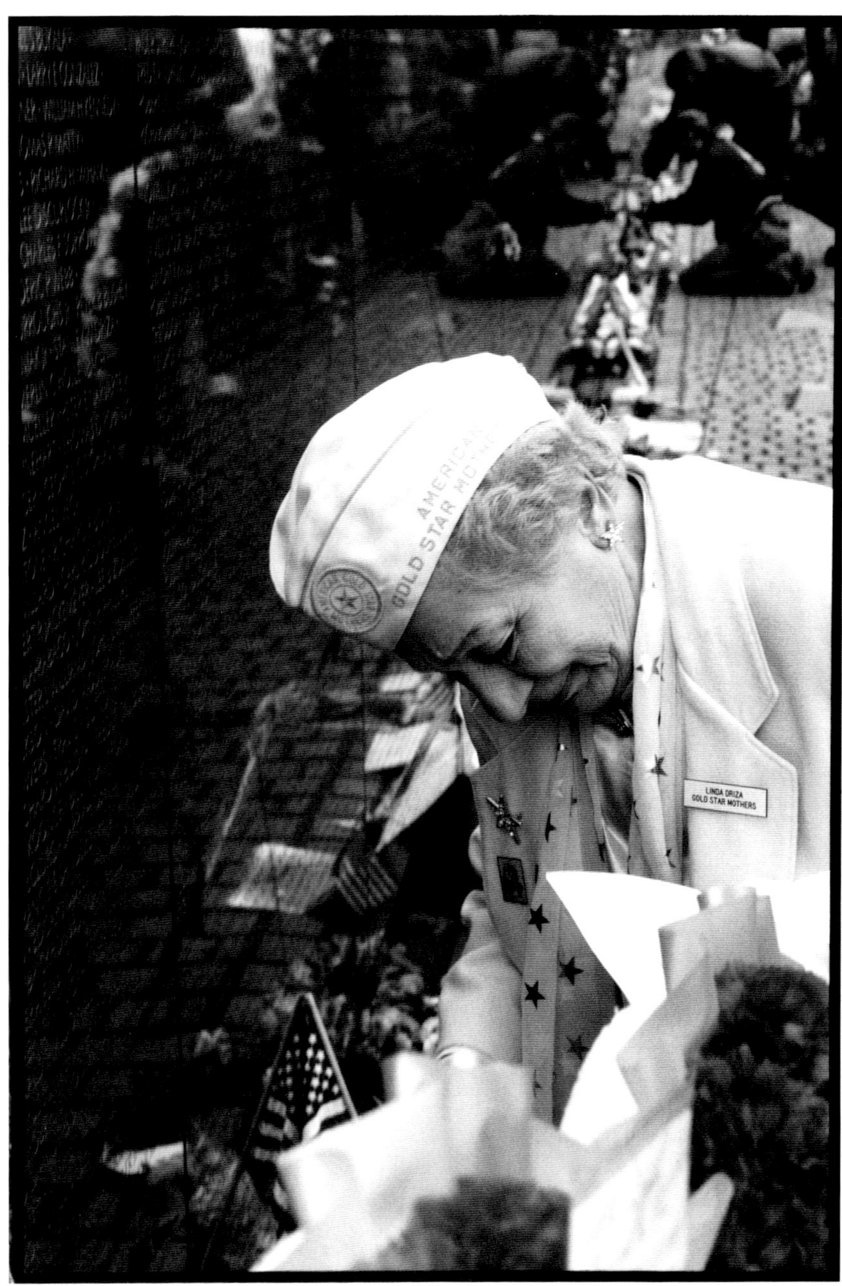

PLATE 49

1992

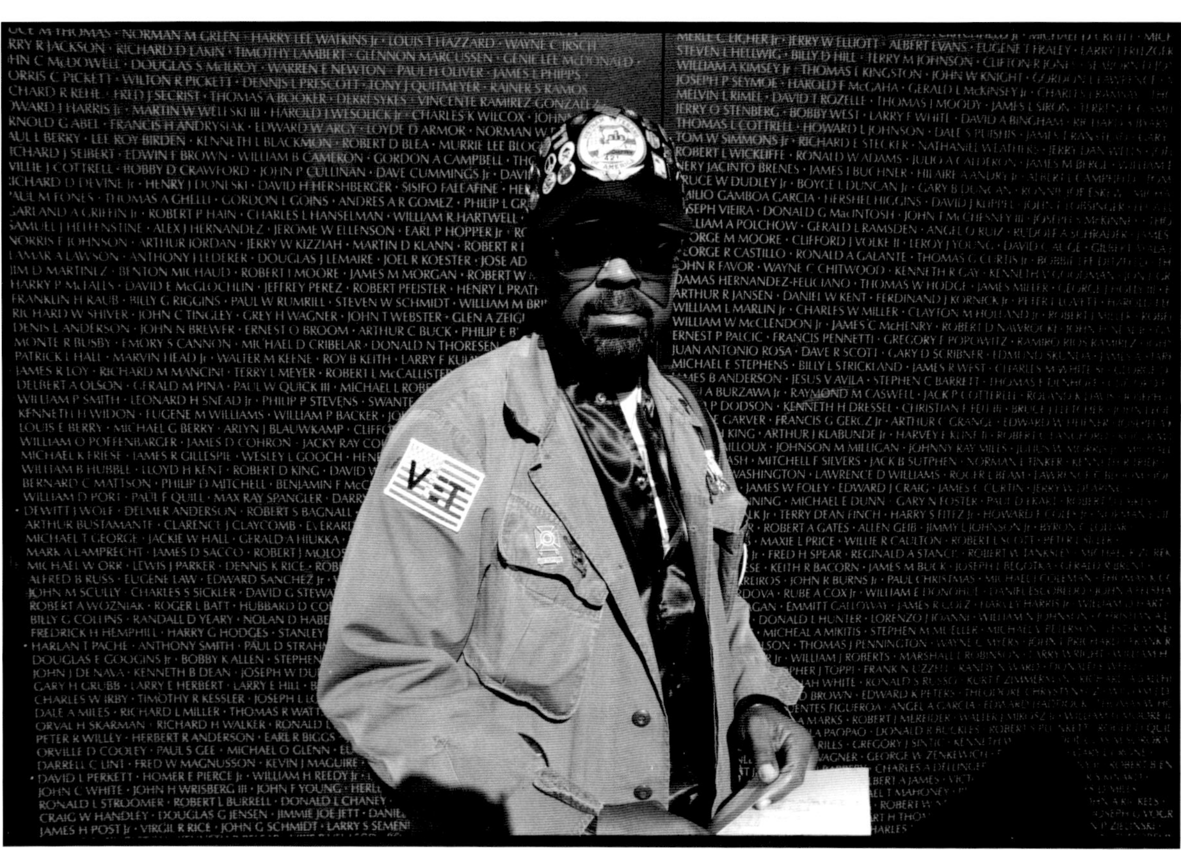

PLATE 50

1985

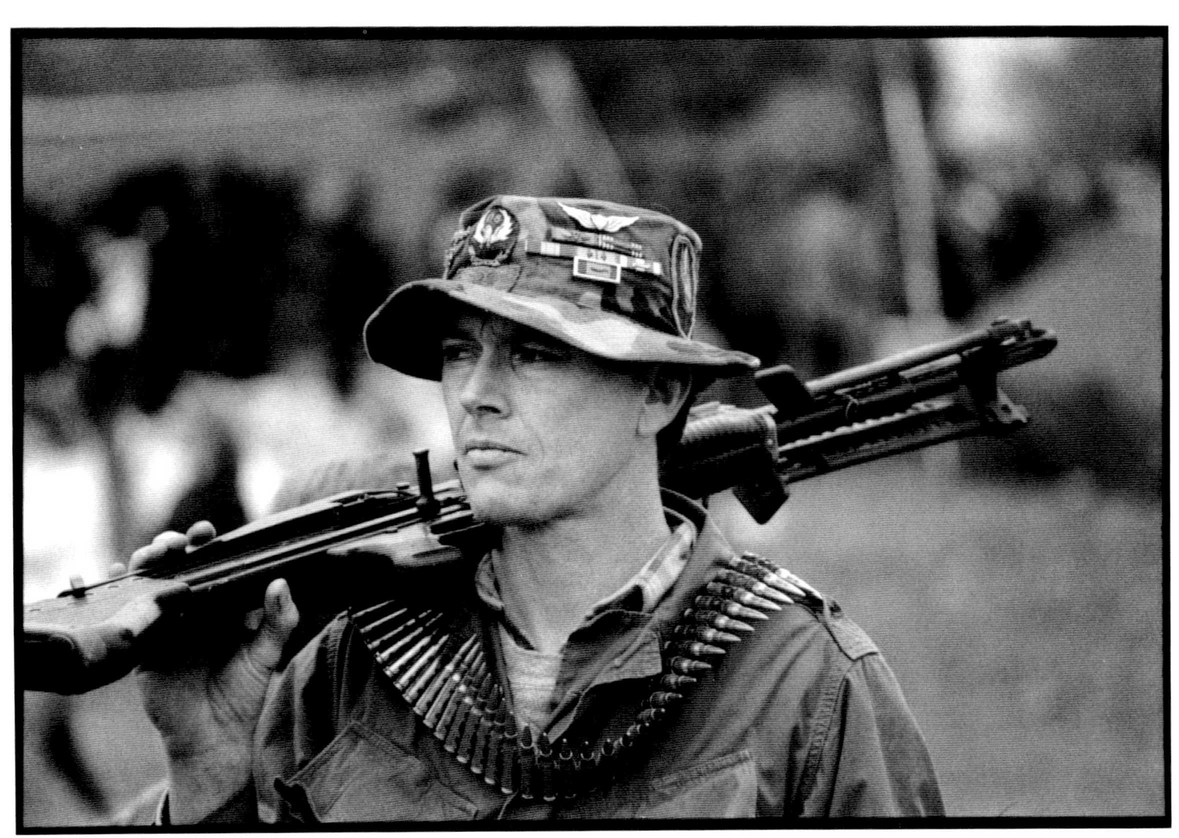

PLATE 51

1992

Dear Harvey,

I passed The Wall yesterday & started sobbing. I couldn't come any closer. Today I'm back to find your name, make a rubbing, to make my amends to you and to grieve. I remember you standing next to the blue Chevy in my driveway . . . you were very brave. I hope seeing your name & leaving this letter will help me heal the conflict inside. I cry at movies about Viet Nam. I cry about my friend Bill who survived. But the nightmares, the depression, the anger continues to destroy his life. Then there's that man I dated for a while in '69. He'd drink himself into a stupor every night & scream over & over again, "Call a dust off!" Maybe you were the lucky one, Harvey.

Harvey, I'm so sorry you died. You would have made a good friend, husband, father. You had the gentlest soul of any man I knew back then. It's just not fair!

Nancy

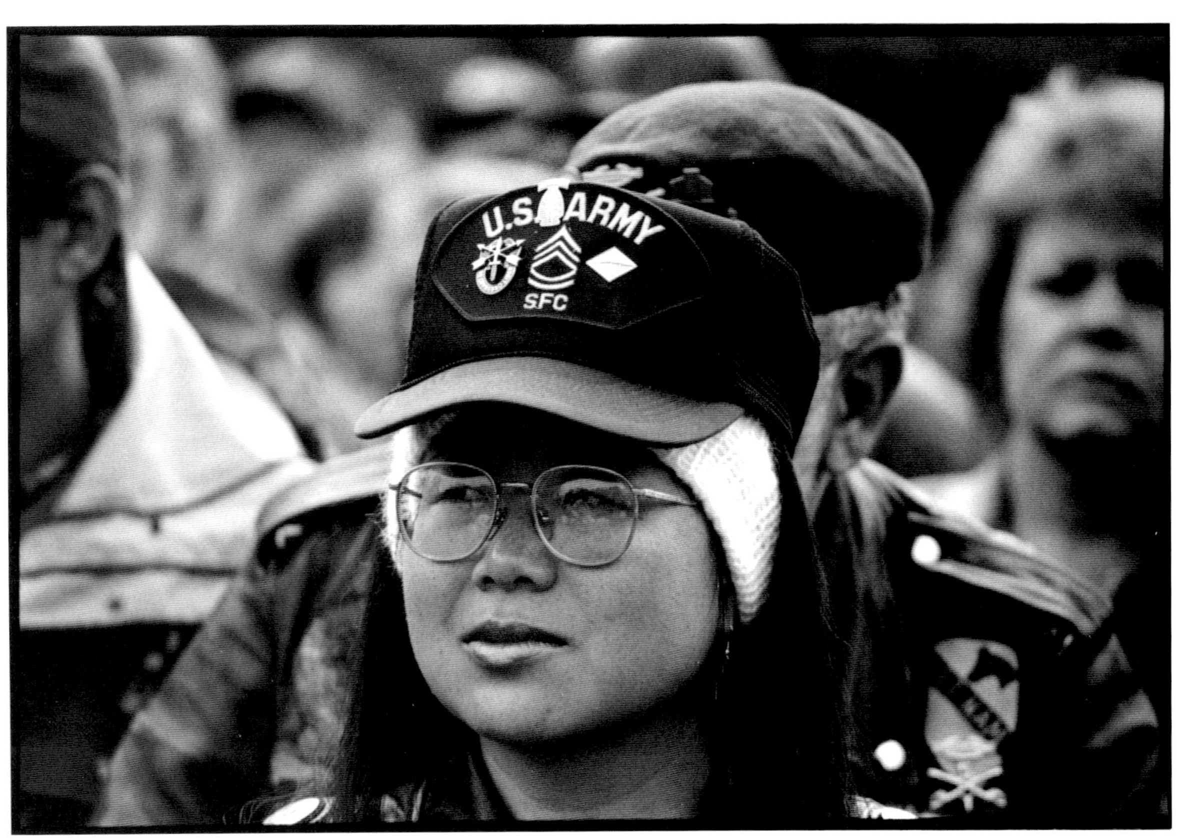

PLATE 52

1996

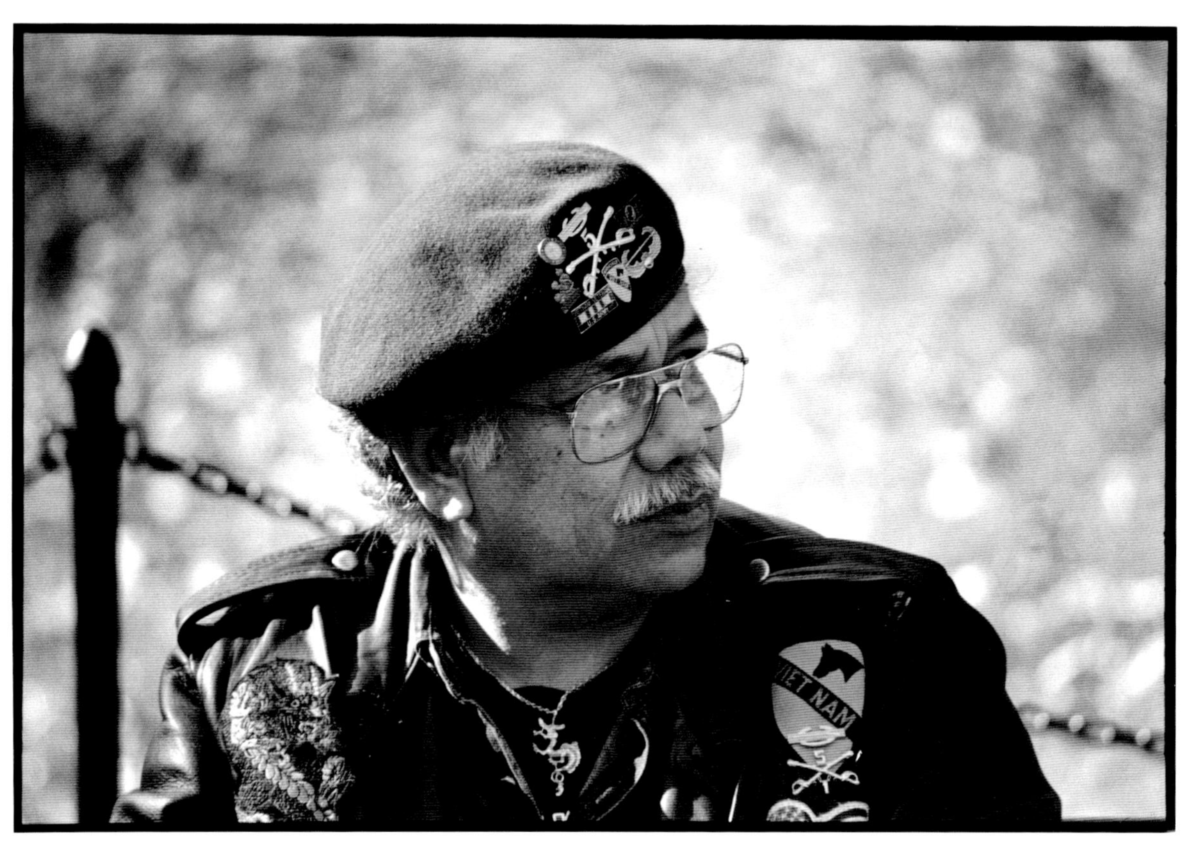

PLATE 53

1990

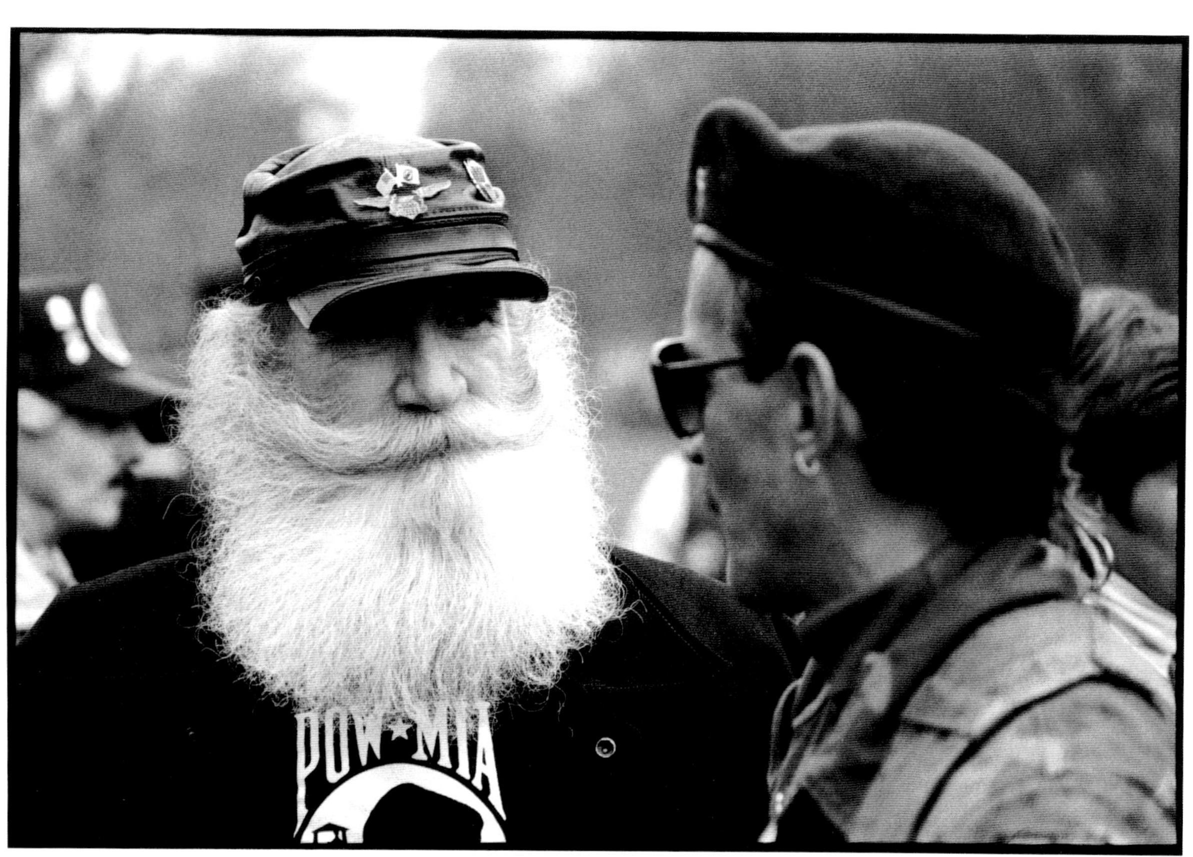

PLATE 54
1996

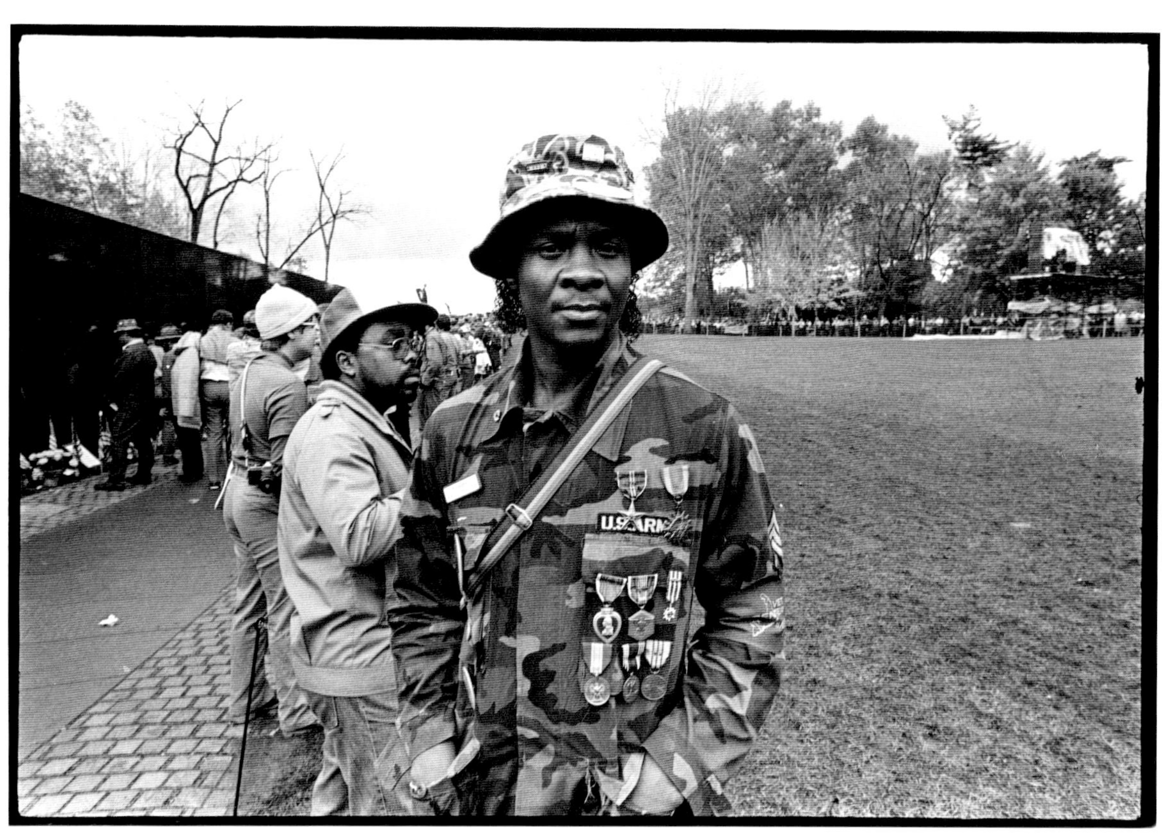

PLATE 55
1986

Joseph,

My Dearest friend of all my high school years—my college years. We grew up together—half way anyway. I'd hoped we could grow old together. How little I knew how dependent I was on you. We could never talk about losing though—the "Conflict" was unpopular—But, oh, how we felt it. How, these past three years the Nation is coming to its senses and recognizing what you and your friends of great courage sacrificed. I knew you to be a man of sensitivity, of honor and full of a sense of responsibility. You went when you didn't have to go—a volunteer—a patriot who believed in your country and accepted the good and the difficult with that belief. I miss you now as much as I missed you then. Your death changed my life in a way I didn't even know until just recently. I will always hold you in a special place in my heart. And you will grow old with me. For you were and always will be a part of my life and our memories do not dim with the passing of time. I have told some friends that this trip to Washington was a Pilgrimage. I am coming here to honor you and the many who gave themselves for their family—friends and country. We have loved you always. And we respect the choices you made. Perhaps some day we'll meet again.

Fondest affections, Aryela
5/29/85

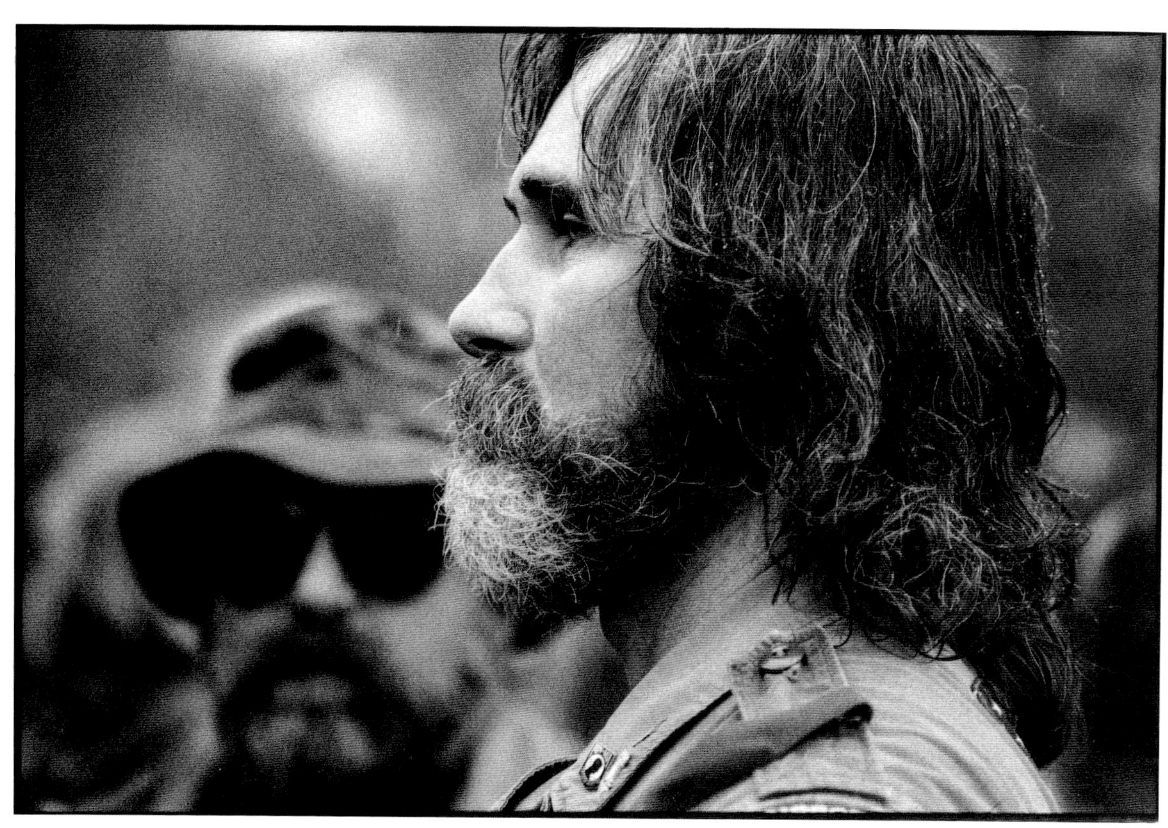

PLATE 56
1985

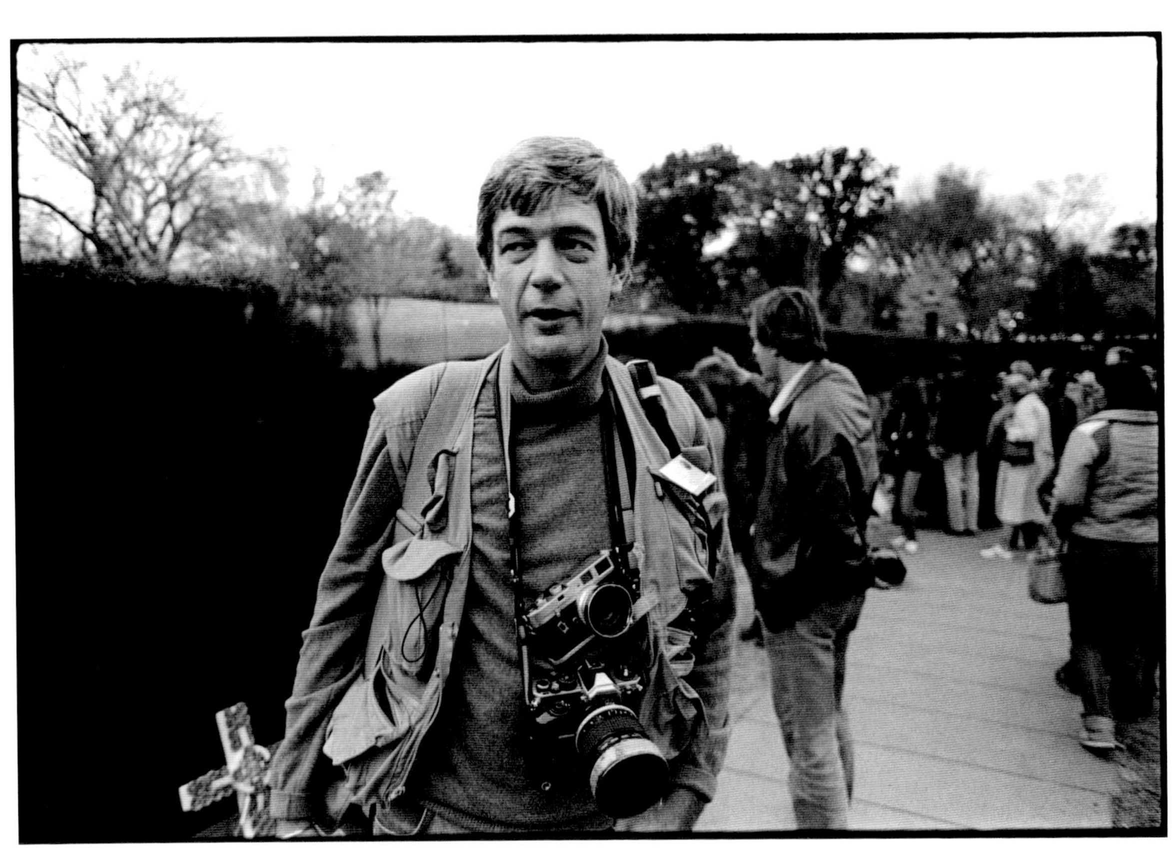

PLATE 57
1983

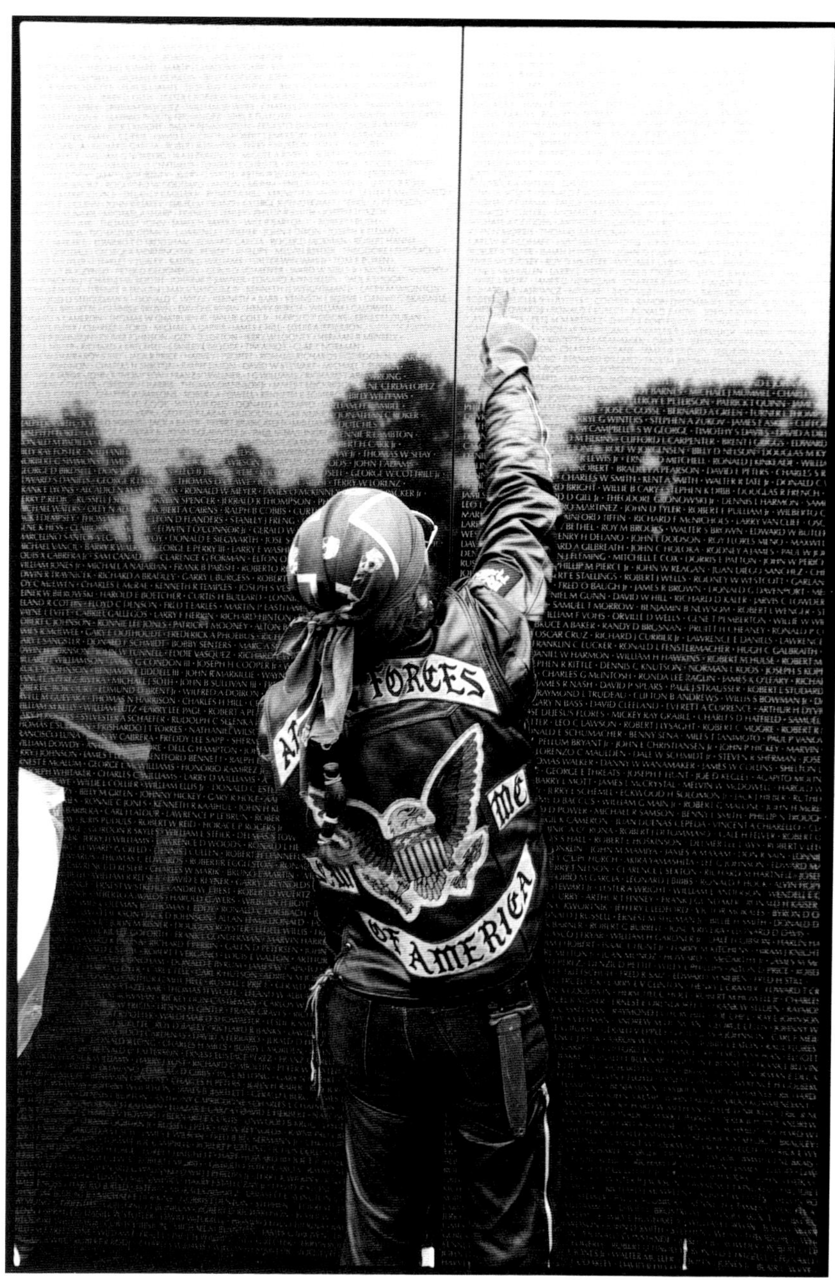

PLATE 58

1988

Because I love you Daddy!

Your daughter
Anne Lynn

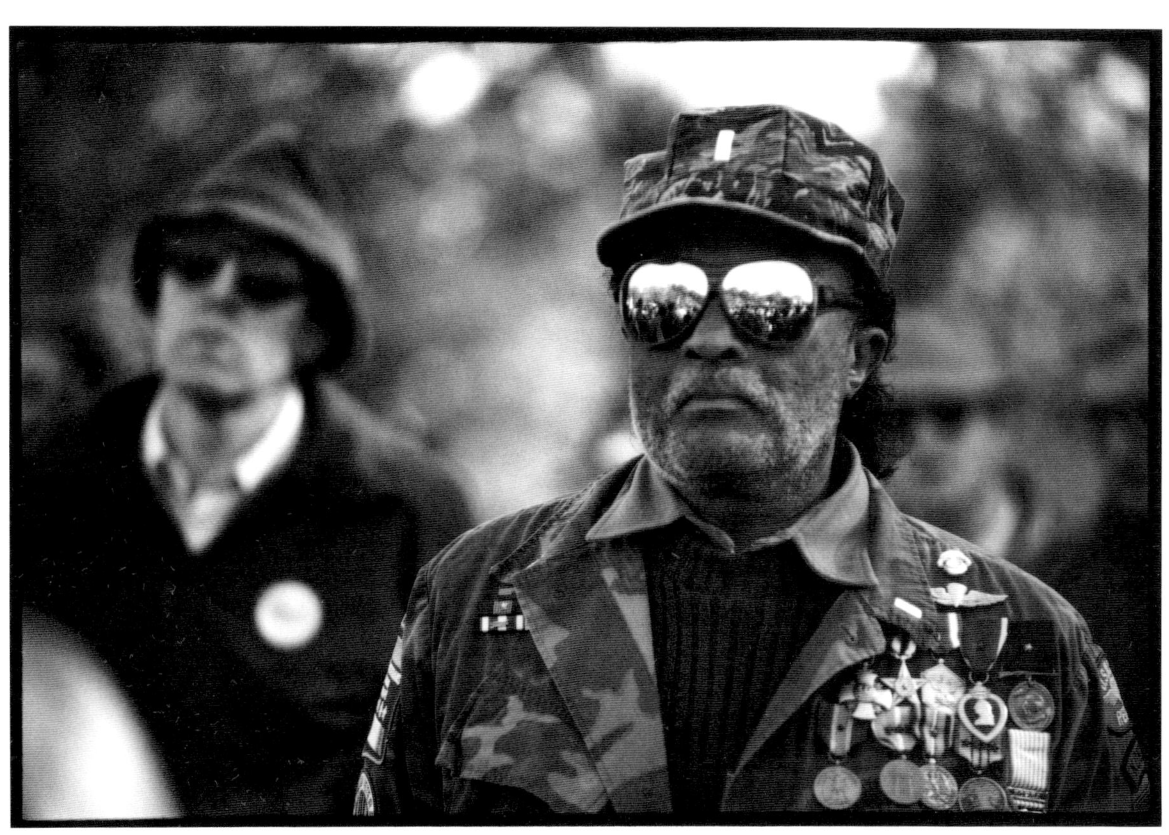

PLATE 59
1993

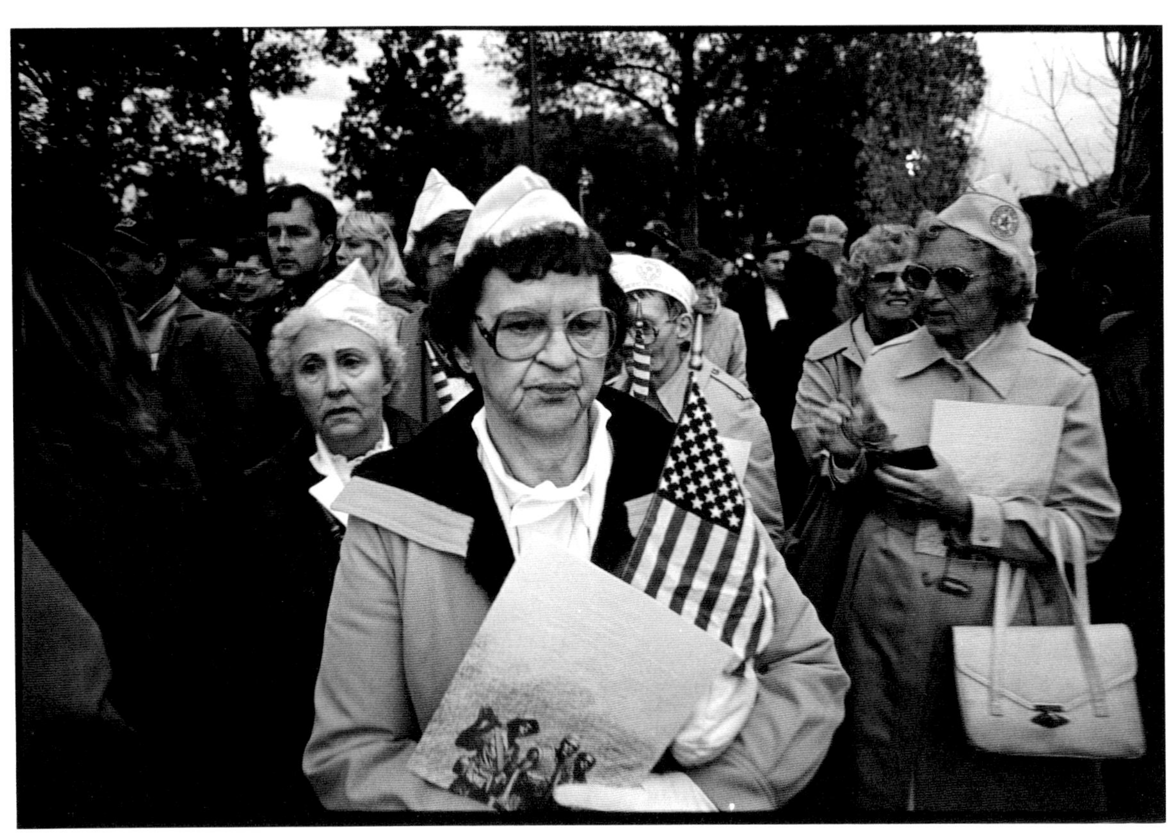

PLATE 60
1983

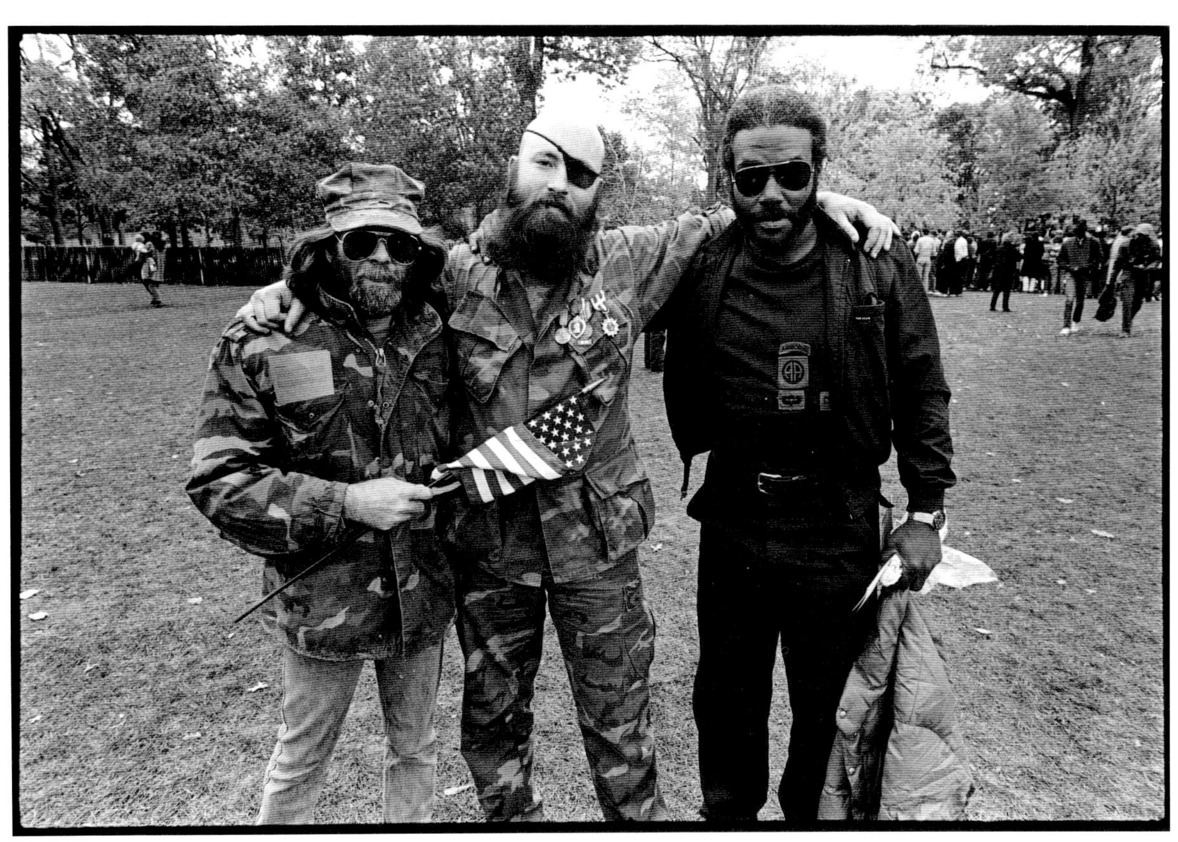

PLATE 61
1984

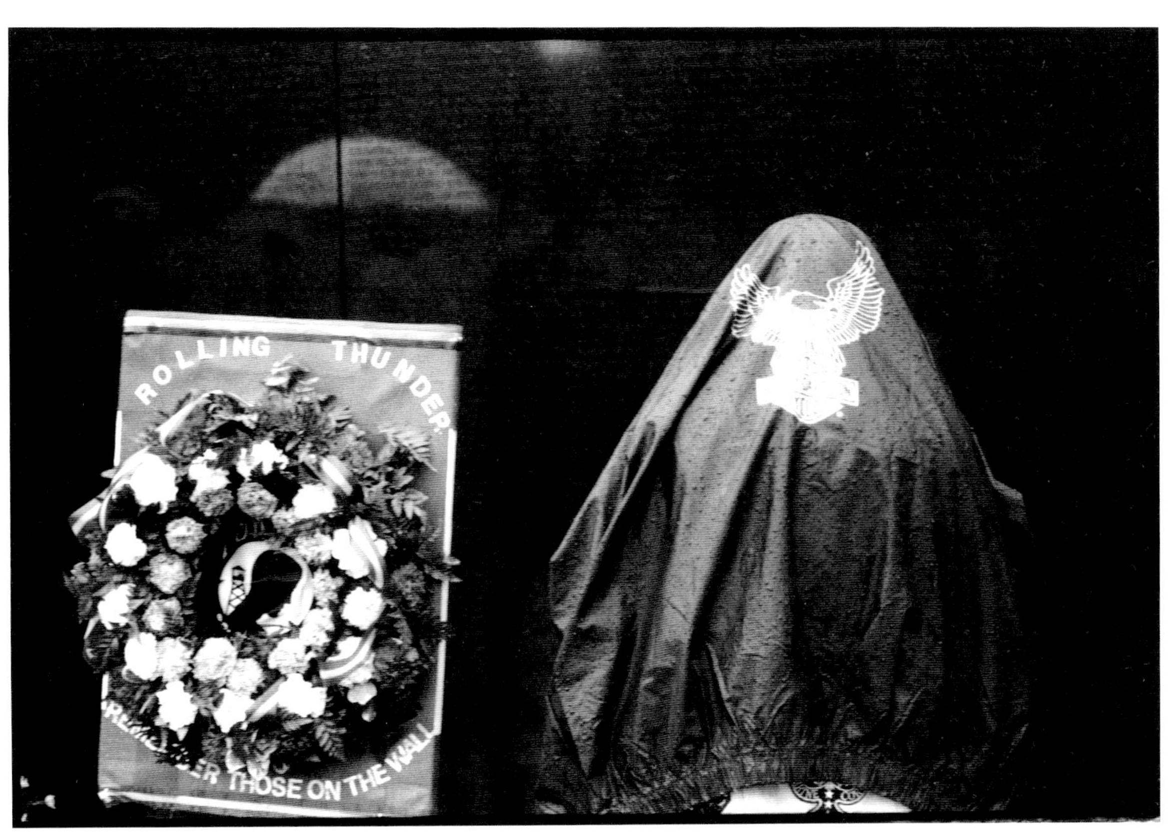

PLATE 62

1996

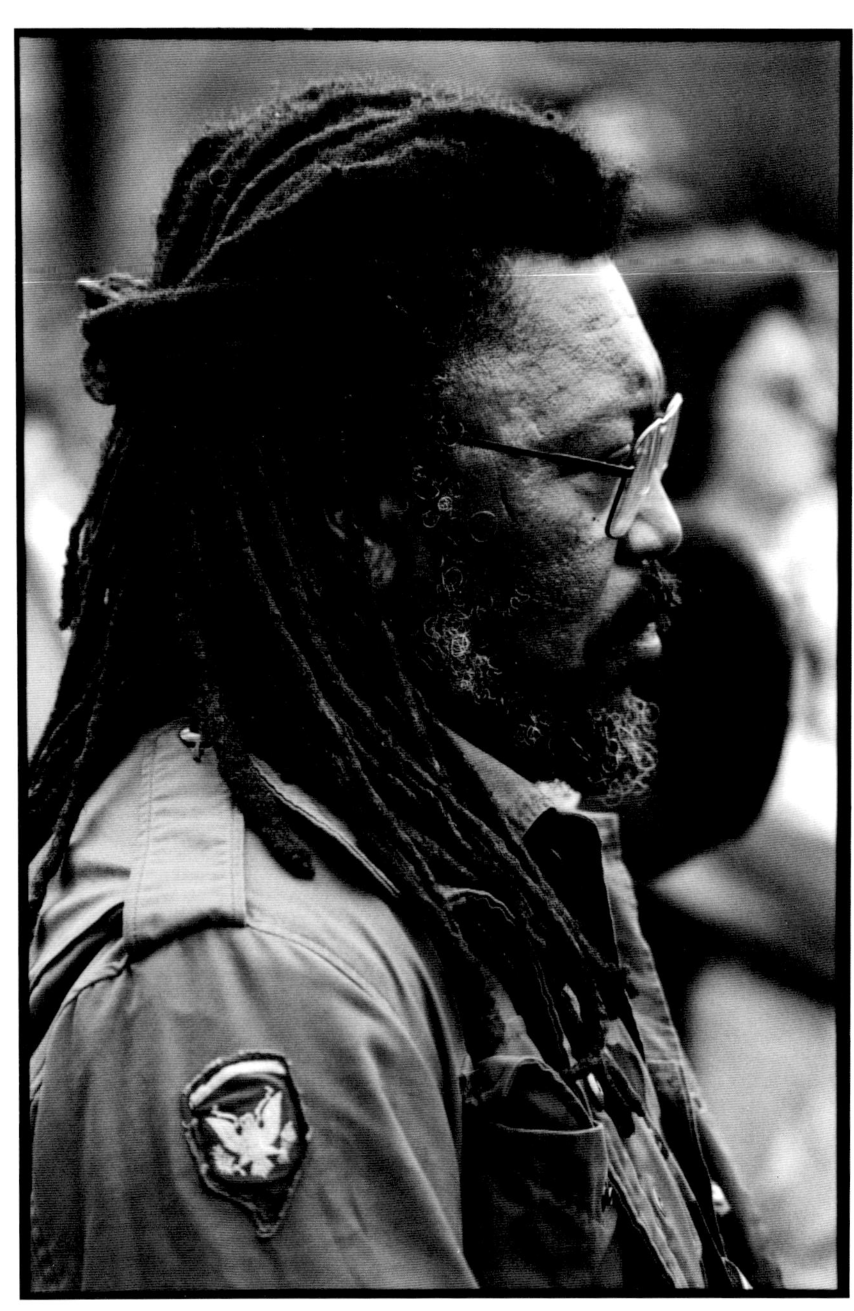

PLATE 63
1990

Goodbye my life line,

For years now I've felt the loneliness, anger, hopelessness and never knew why. Now at the door of fifty, I remember a young kid, happy, free and bold. He was in Viet-Nam, yet I felt in love with this place, its fierceness even its danger. Maybe I was too stupid to be afraid. All I know is it was in my body, my soul, my mind. I loved this place called Viet-Nam. The danger, the heart break, the fear of death all made my adrenaline flow. When my time came to go home, I said no, and stayed another tour. I was a junkie for this strange land. I grew to manhood overnight, gave up all the teenage games and dreams, but I gave them up freely. Why did I have to go? I love you Viet-Nam.

Ernie
1998

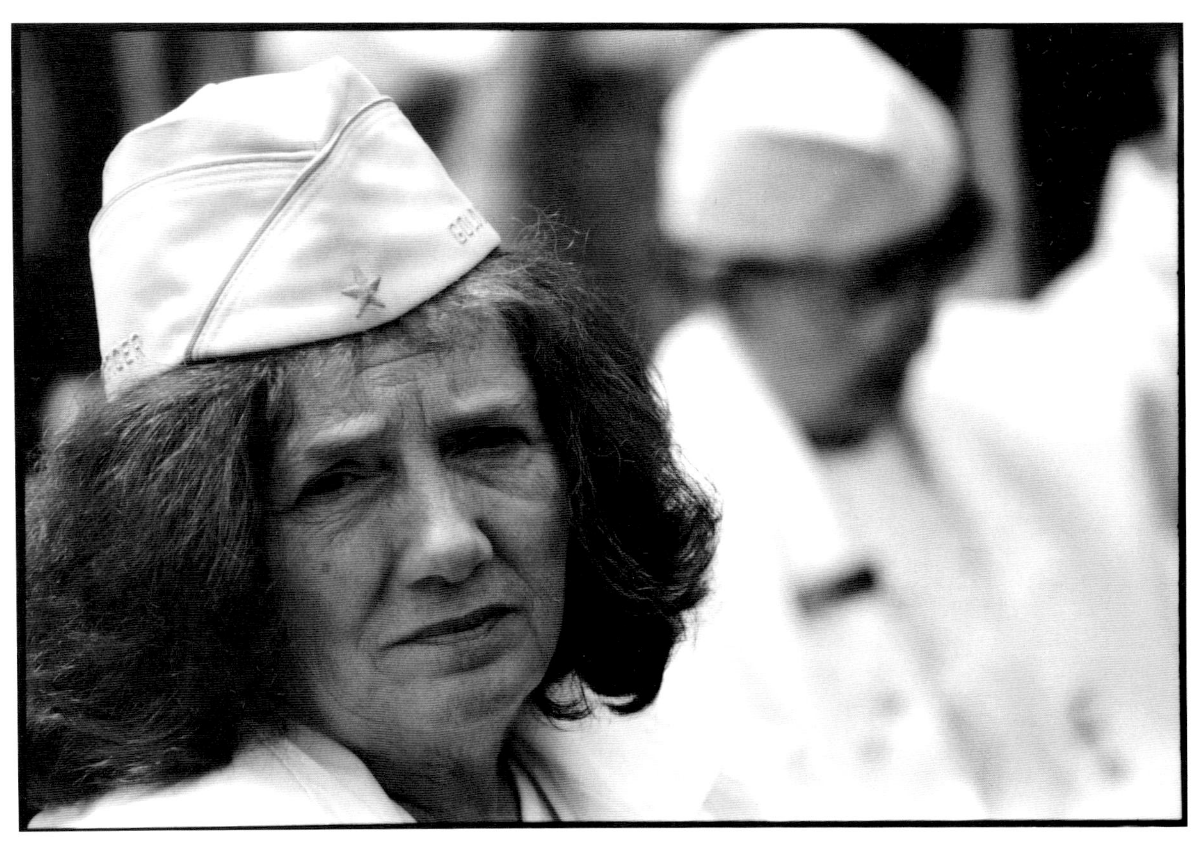

PLATE 64
1995

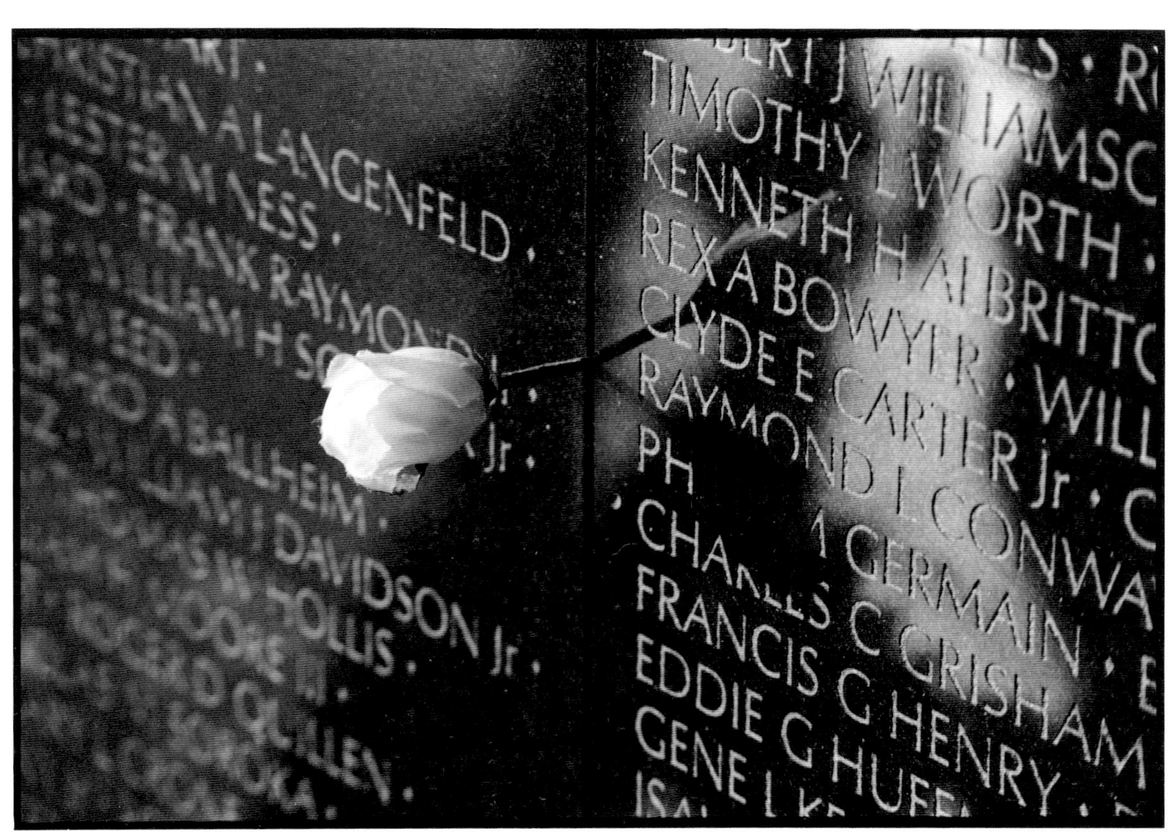

PLATE 65

1989

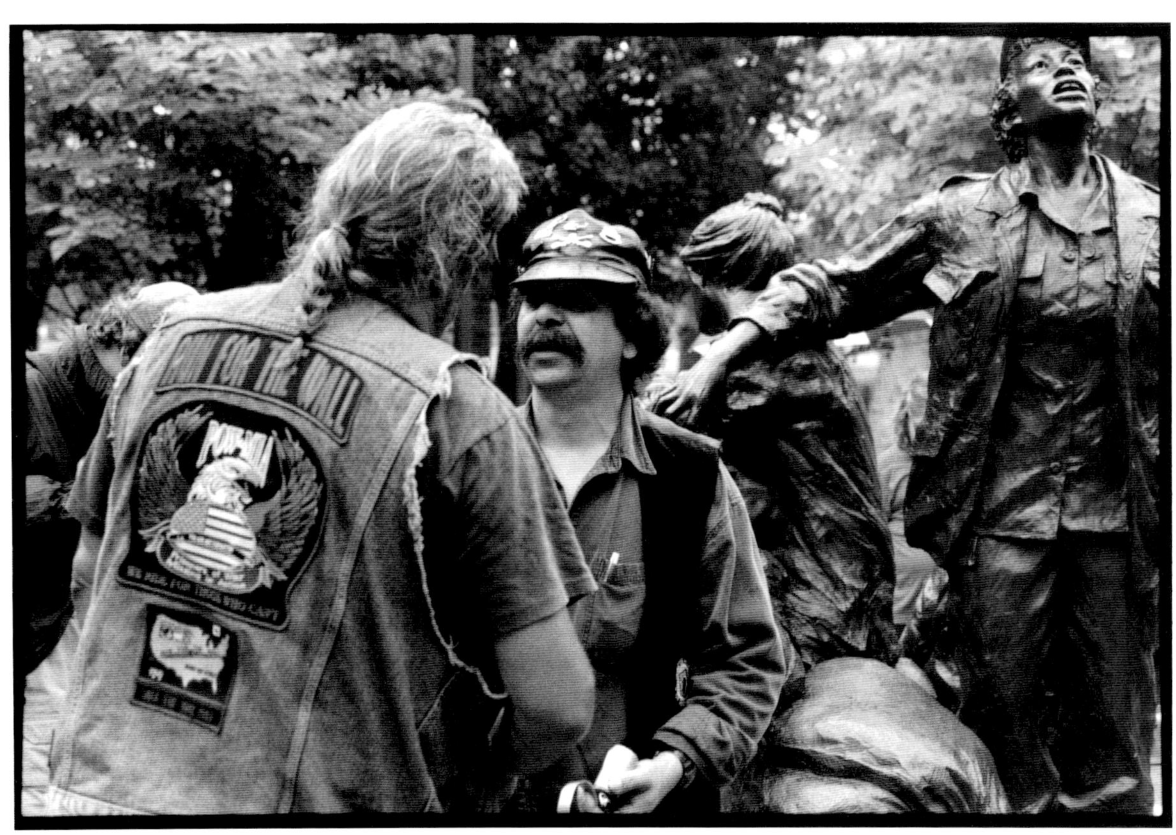

PLATE 66
1994

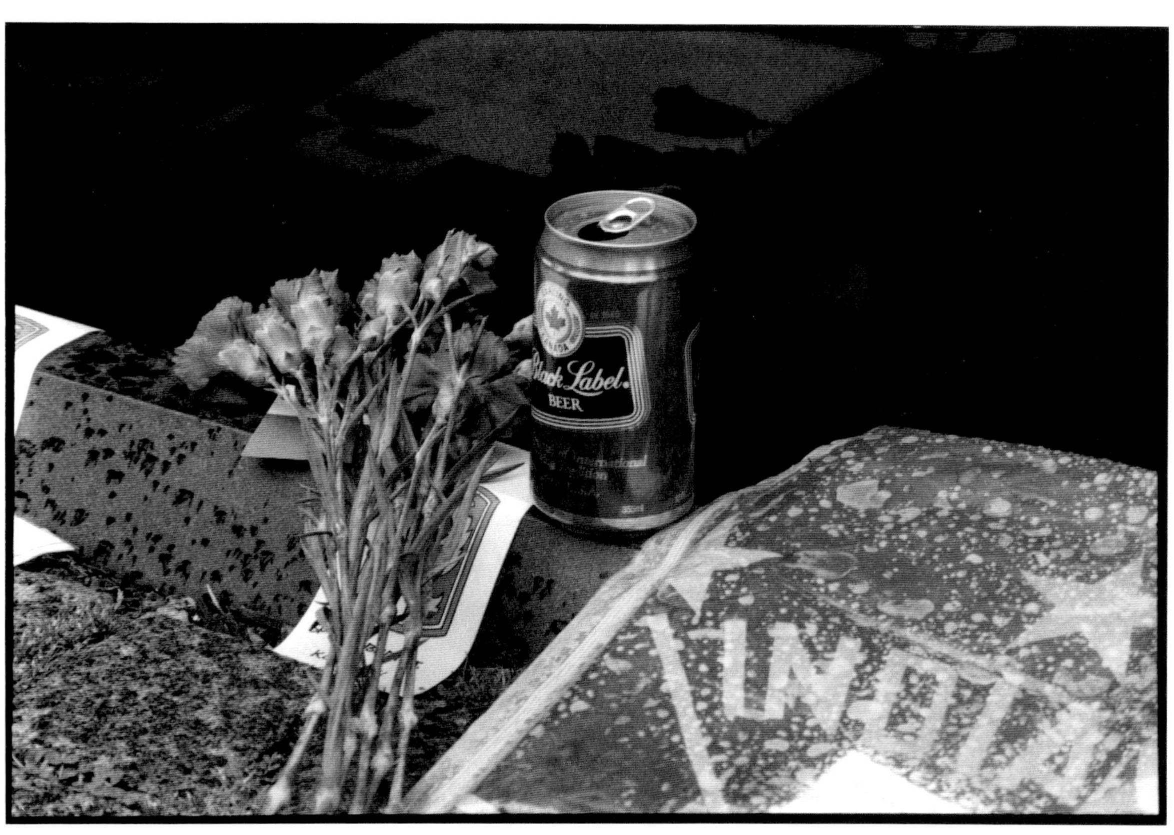

PLATE 67

1987

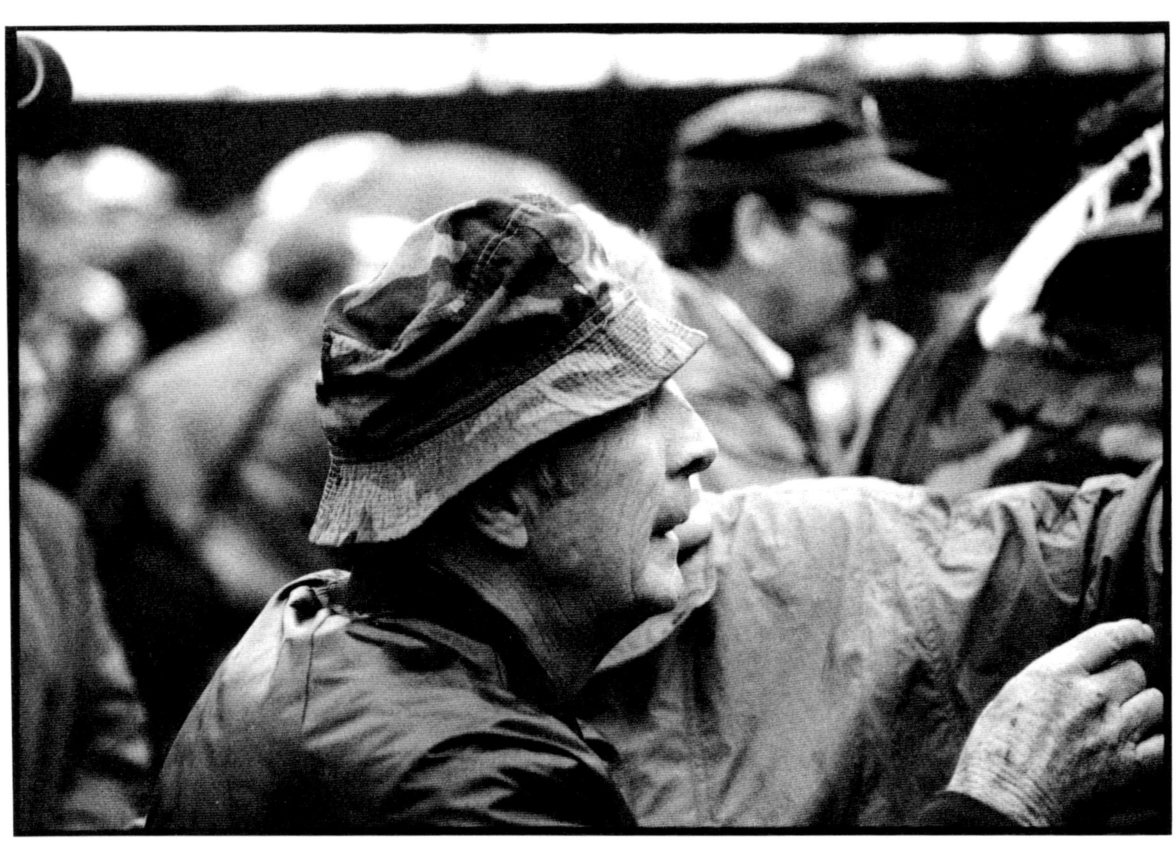

PLATE 68
1990

Dear Tony,

I want to finish up some business between us. I want you to know how much you hurt me by us not getting married. All these years it felt like such a rejection, like you just didn't love me enough to marry me, yet I realize now in your mind it was because you did love me so much, you felt by marrying me you would only hurt me more if you were to die, like you did. I'm really mad at you for dying on me, you know how much I loved you, maybe we should have broken ties before you went over! Oh who am I kidding (only myself). When you died I lost part of me you know you were my life.

Well Honey, I haven't lived the last 26 years in peace I must let you go and rest in peace with God where I know you are.

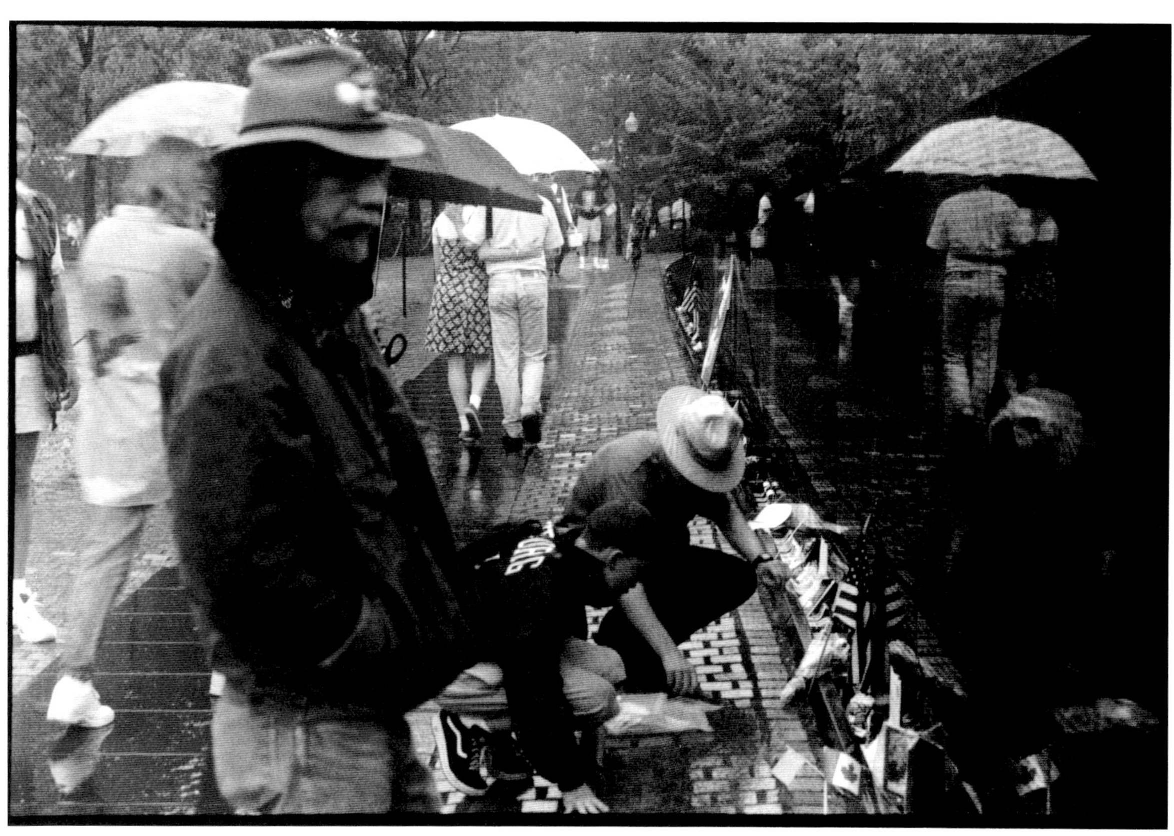

PLATE 69

1996

In our family, in our home and in our lives, the Vietnam war will never end. There is no enemy that you can see. There are no weapons, no fighting, no hardships. Only an emptiness because a loved one is missing and the never ending questions of why? . . . he took his laughter, his jokes and his love for life and went to that far away country. Flying away, late one night from the ones who loved him. . . . Where did he go, this young son of mine, who was so full of life . . . and where is he now? Now he is just a memory . . .

I'm the one who held and rocked him as a baby. I'm the one who kissed away the hurts. I'm the one who taught him right from wrong. I'm the one who cried when Uncle Sam said, "I want you." I'm the one who hugged and kissed him for the last time and watched him fly away from me, to war. I'm the one who prayed each night. "Dear God, keep him safe." And I'm the goofy Mom who sent a Christmas tree to him in Vietnam. I'm also the one whose heart broke when told this big young son of mine had died in that far away country called Vietnam. And I'm the one who still cries because of all the memories of him that will never die. So, Vietnam, Vietnam what did you take from me?

But how many people know the tragedy of that war still goes on for the 2,482 American men . . . these men are listed as P.O.W./M.I.A, but they are more than that. They are human beings . . . husbands, Sons, fathers, brothers and much, much more. Please help to get these men home and end this suffering for them and their loved ones.

(Written by a Mother who lost her son in Vietnam but still cares about the ones who are still unaccounted for.)

Eleanor

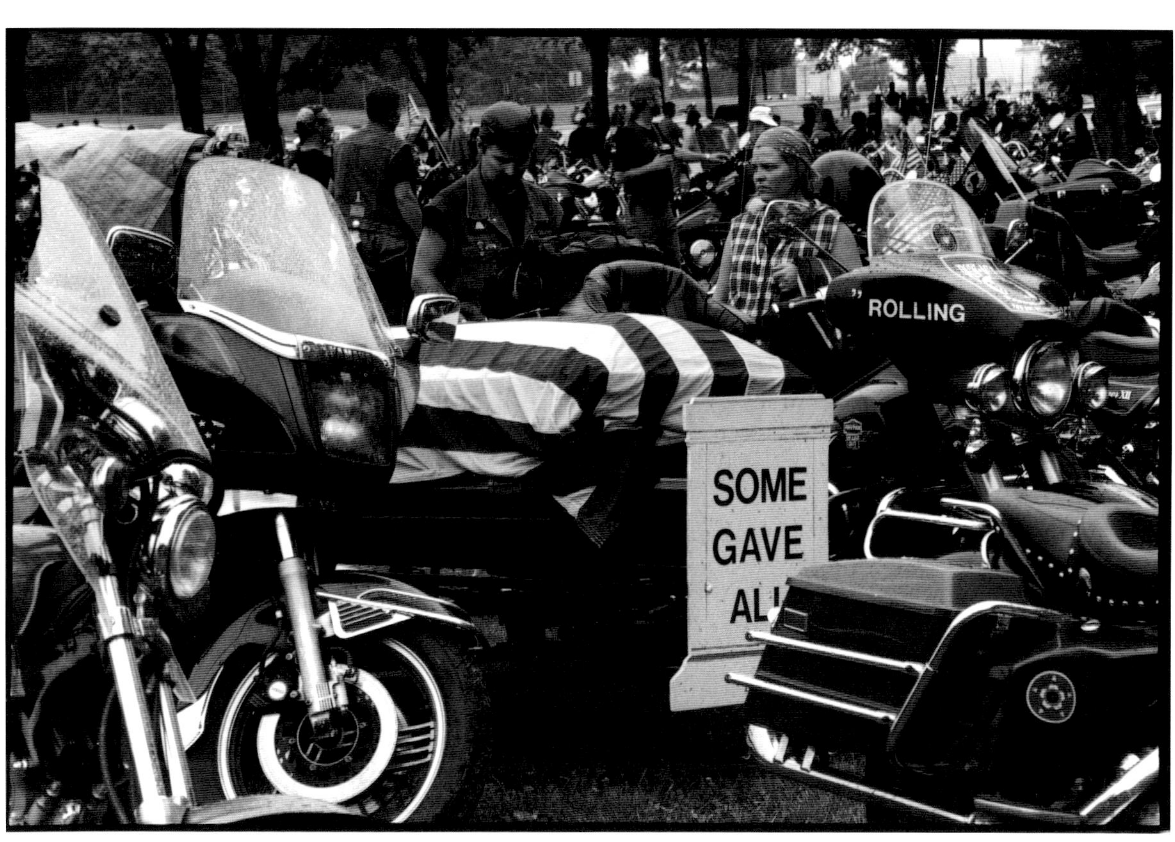

PLATE 70
1996

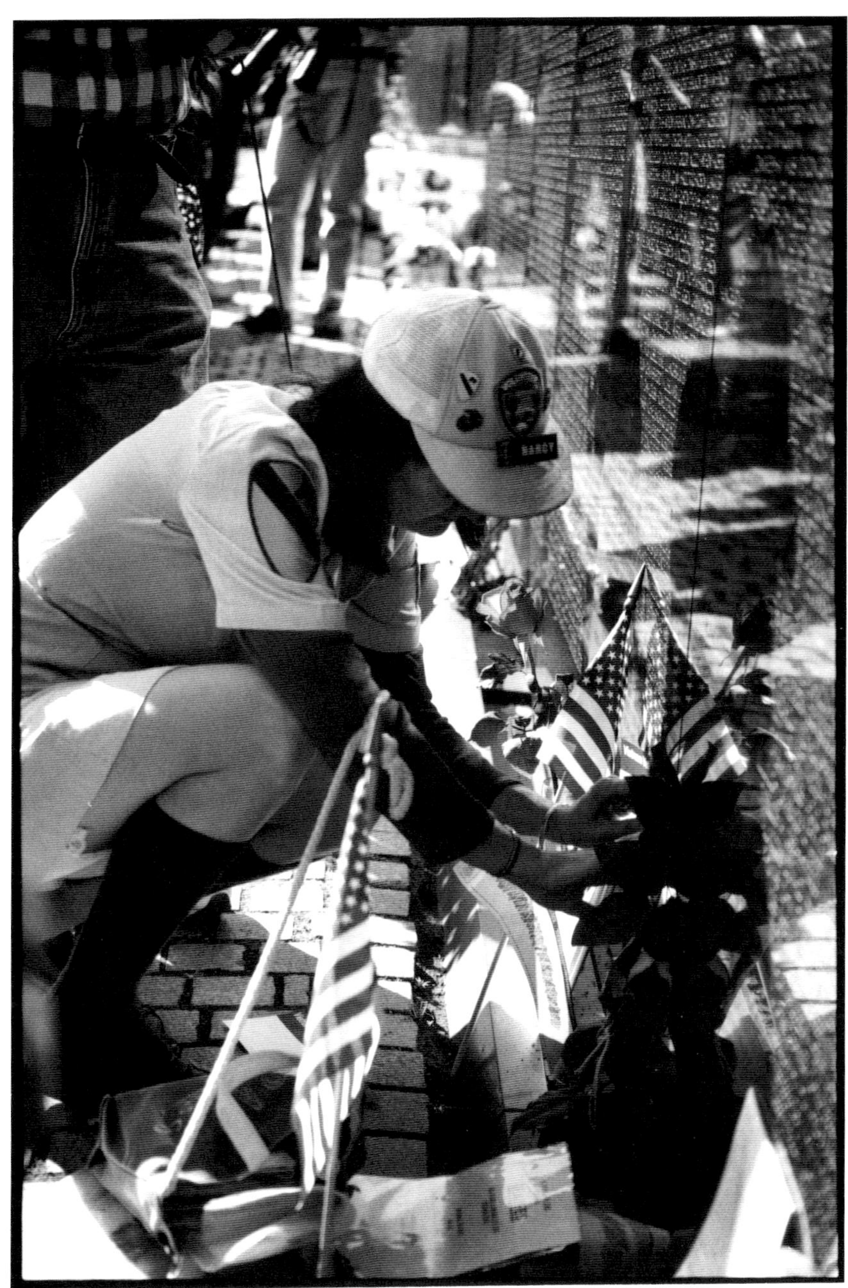

PLATE 71

1999

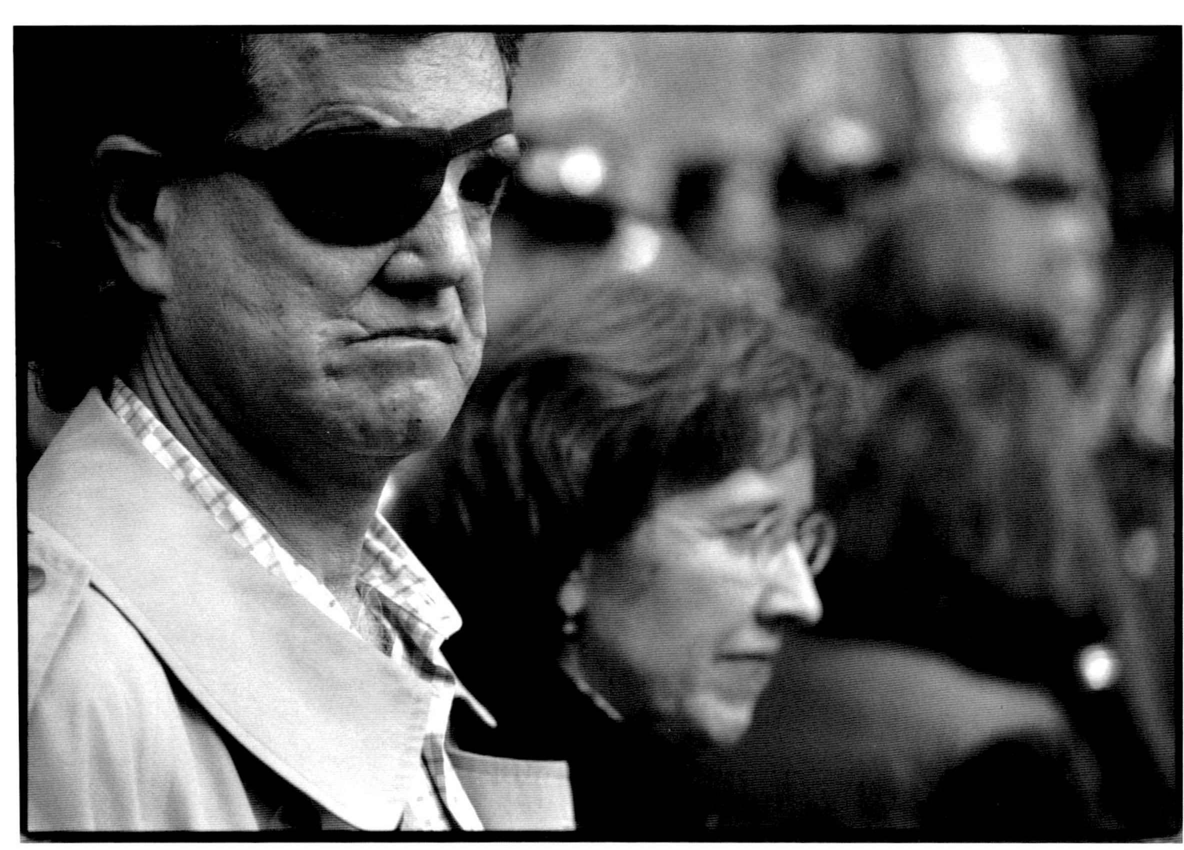

PLATE 72
1999

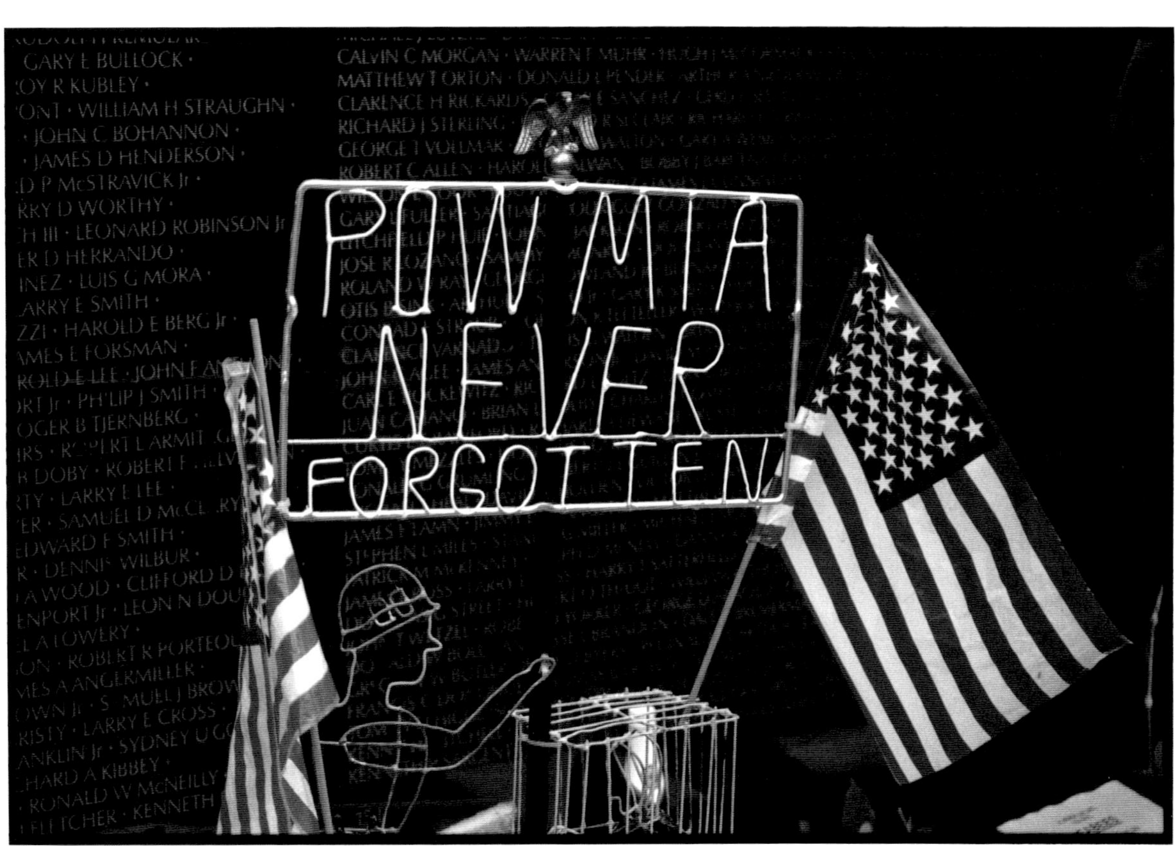

PLATE 73

1999

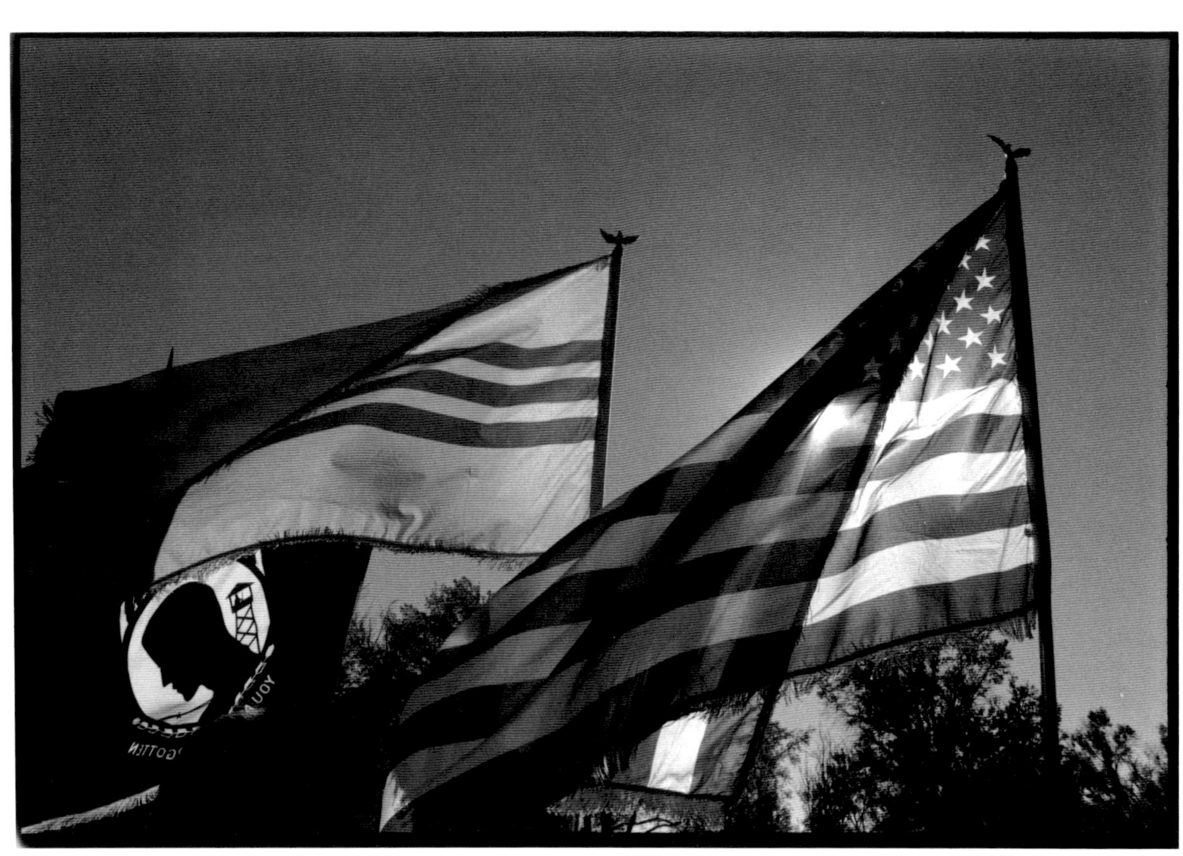

PLATE 74

1999

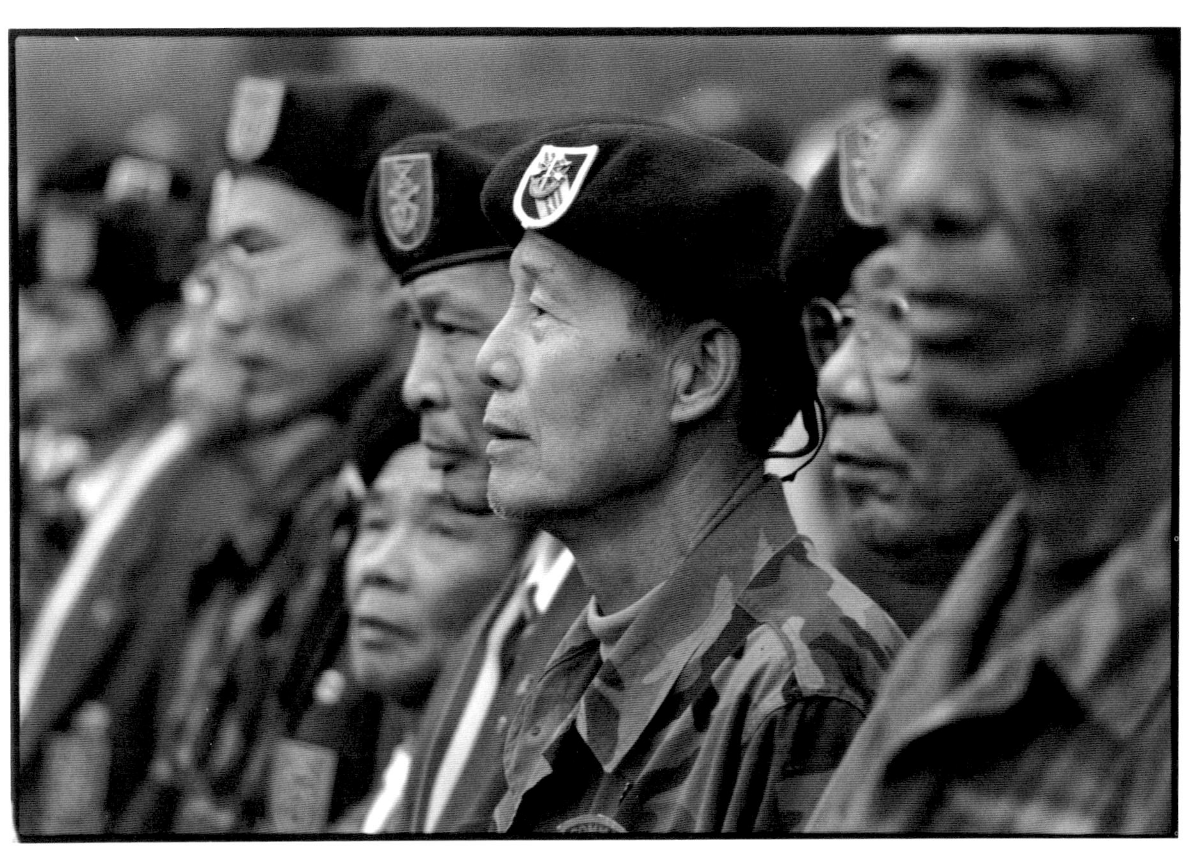

PLATE 75
1999

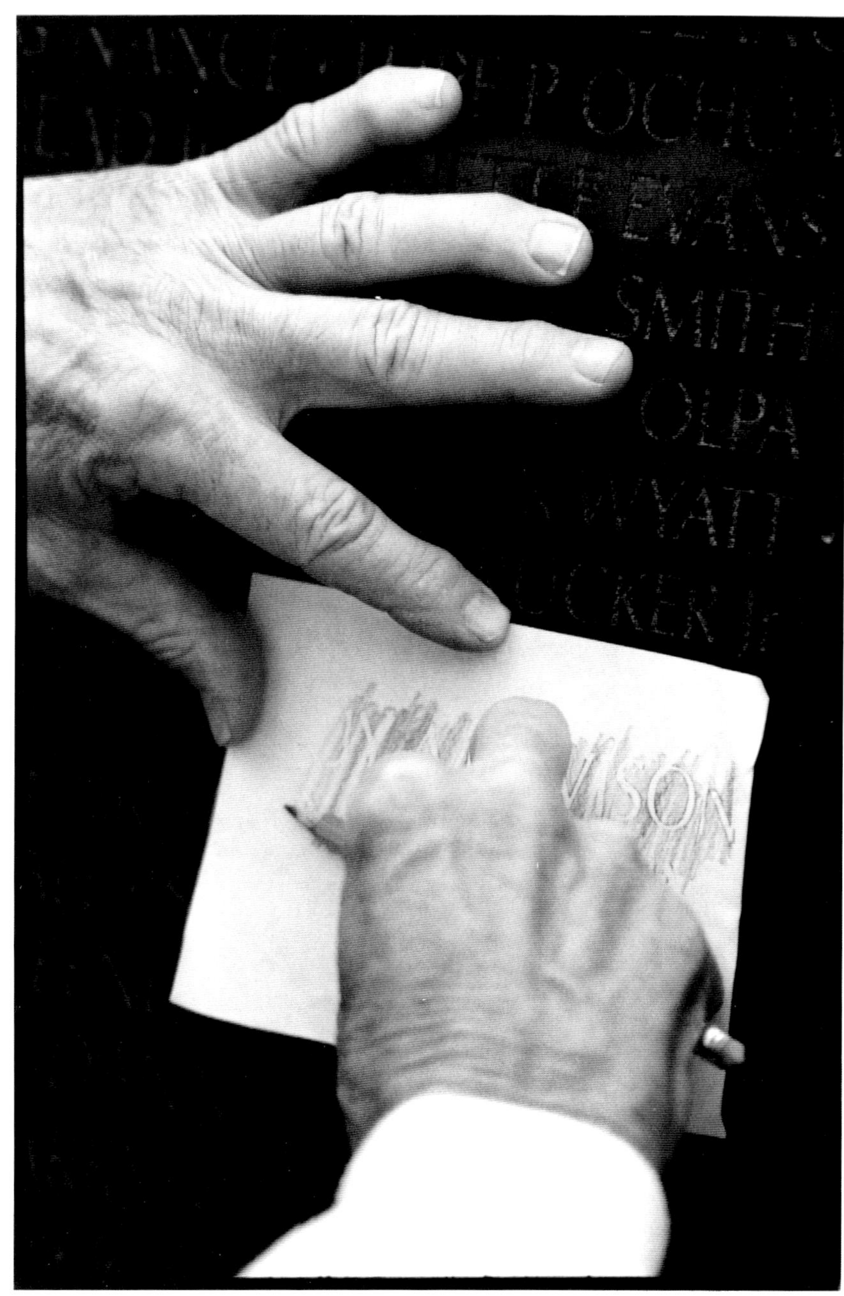

PLATE 76
1990

Lance,

I come to see you over and over again. It has been almost 30 years for me since I shared the battlefields of Vietnam with you my friend. The wounds in my heart have subsided to a quieter place in my mind, but my memory of you has not faded.

I often catch myself still wondering why I was chosen and allowed to live. Such a random act. My surviving to return home, a chance happening for which I thank God who made us. I pray for all of our souls. Torn from our friends and loved ones at such an early age, may we all rest in peace in the end.

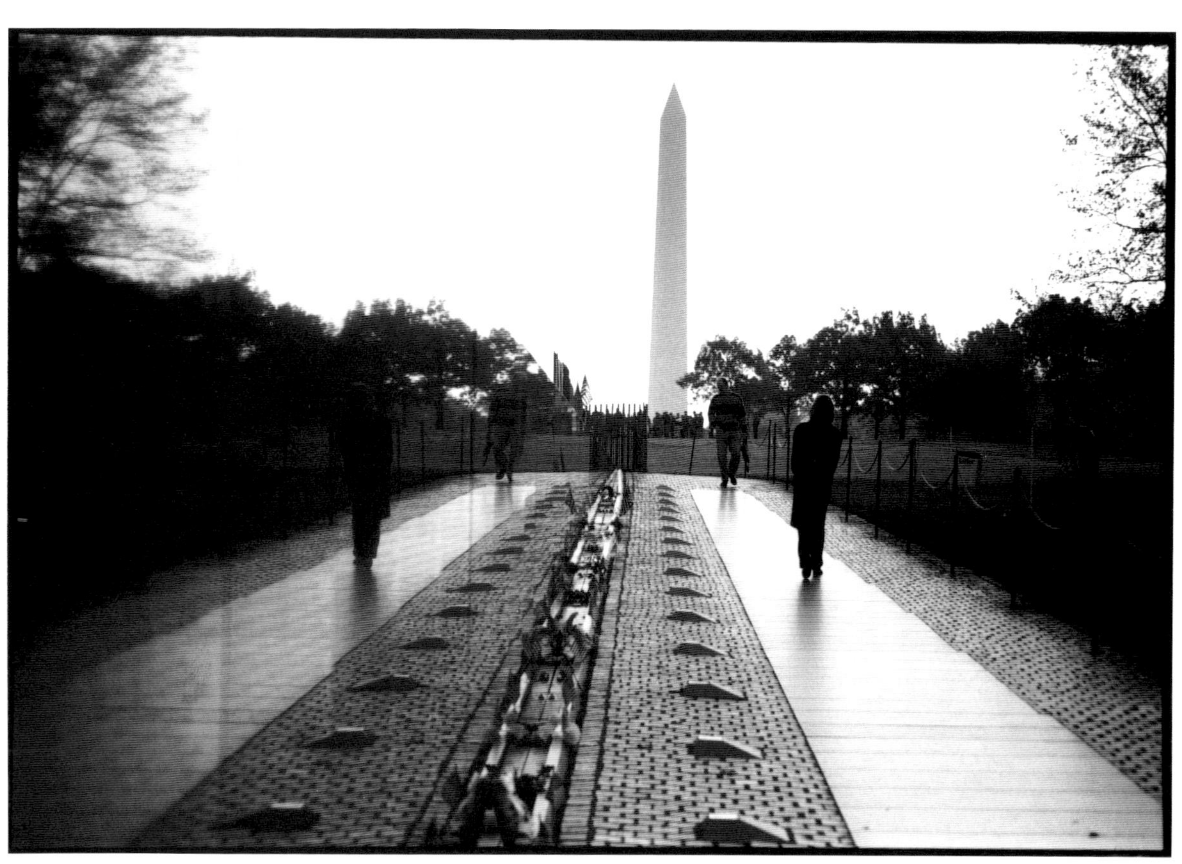

PLATE 77
1998

Acknowledgments

Thanks to my wife, Sandra, for her ongoing love, help, and support. I am grateful to Adrian Cronauer, Jan Craig Scruggs, Jerry Uelsmann, Gordon Parks, Dr. Franklin Robinson, Leonard Lang, Lang Photo, Color Lab Inc., Lily Packer, Dr. José Neistein, Durey Felton, Dr. Peter Rollins, Hon. J. Eldon Yates, Libby Hatch, the Rhode Island State Council on the Arts, and the Vietnam Veterans Institute; without their support over the years this book would not be possible. I thank Syracuse University Press. And I extend my special thanks to all those whose images I have captured at The Wall through the years—this is your book as well.

THOMAS F. MORRISSEY served in Vietnam in 1970–71 as a helicopter pilot with the 117th Assault Helicopter Company. A decorated combat veteran, he flew combat assaults and night missions along the Ho Chi Minh Trail. Morrissey is professor of fine arts and communications, and is a professional photographer, digital imager, and filmmaker. He has taught at the Massachusetts Institute of Technology, the Rhode Island School of Design, University of Brasilia, and Mendicino Art Center. He has photographed for PLAN International, Child Find, USIS, Partners of the Americas, and USAID and has been awarded the Kellogg International Fellowship in Community Development. His images are included in several major collections, including the Corcoran Gallery, the International Center for Photography, the Herbert Johnson Museum of Art at Cornell University, the Rhode Island School of Design Museum of Art, and the Vietnam Veterans Museum of Art.

JAN CRAIG SCRUGGS served as an army infantryman in Vietnam. He is the founder and president of the Vietnam Veterans Memorial Fund.

ADRIAN CRONAUER is senior attorney and corporate vice president of Burch and Cronauer and is a specialist in communications law. He served in Vietnam as an Air Force Sergeant and radio personality for Armed Forces Vietnam Radio (AFVN). He is co-author of the original autobiographical story for the motion picture *Good Morning, Vietnam,* starring Robin Williams.